CULTURES OF THE WORLD®

PERU

Kieran Falconer & Lynette Quek

Marshall Cavendish Benchmark

NEW YORK

PICTURE CREDITS

Cover photo: © Art Wolfe / Danita Delimont Stock Photography
alt.TYPE / Reuters: 27, 28, 29, 32, 33, 39, 44, 80, 85, 122 • Bjorn Klingwall: 54 (top), 72, 77, 95 • Buddy Mays: 5, 43, 50
• Corel Stock Photo Library: 8, 13, 59 • Douglas Donne Bryant: 3, 14, 18, 25, 54 (bottom), 61, 83 (bottom), 96, 103, 107, 113,
125 • Focus Team: 30, 34, 47, 108 • Getty Images: 6, 16, 114 • HBL Network Photo Agency: 92 • Hulton Deutsch: 24, 82
• Life File: 12, 31, 58, 86, 102 • Lonely Planet Images: 1, 46, 64, 90, 96, 106 • MCIA: 45 • Minden Pictures / Frans Lanting: 48
• Photobank / Photolibrary: 7, 19, 21, 83 (top), 93, 117 • Photolibrary.com: 53, 100 • Pietro Scozzari: 42, 112, 128, 130, 131
• Richard I'Anson: 4, 10, 56, 61, 62, 65, 84, 101, 111, 115, 119, 127 • Robert Pateman: 51, 67, 71, 94, 126 • Susana Burton: 79
• The Hutchison Library: 9, 11, 15 (top), 17, 23, 26, 37, 38, 41, 55, 63, 66, 68, 73, 74, 75, 81, 85, 88, 97, 98, 99, 100, 105, 109,
116, 123, 124 • The Image Bank: 15 (bottom), 35, 36, 40, 52, 57, 71, 110, 118, 120 • Veronique Sanson: 76, 89, 121

PRECEDING PAGE

Traditionally dressed indigenous children smile for the camera.

Editorial Director (U.S.): Michelle Bisson
Editors: Deborah Grahame, Mabelle Yeo, Magdalene Koh
Copyreader: Daphne Hougham
Designers: Jailani Basari, Sean Lee
Cover picture researcher: Connie Gardner
Picture researchers: Thomas Khoo, Joshua Ang

Marshall Cavendish Benchmark
99 White Plains Road
Tarrytown, NY 10591
Web site: www.marshallcavendish.us

Originated and designed by Times Editions
An imprint of Marshall Cavendish International (Asia) Private Limited
A member of Times Publishing Limited

All Internet sites were correct and accurate at the time of printing. All monetary figures in this publication are in U.S. dollars.

Library of Congress Cataloging-in-Publication Data
Falconer, Kieran, 1970–
    Peru / by Kieran Falconer and Lynette Quek. — 2nd ed.
       p. cm. —— (Cultures of the world)
    Summary: "Provides comprehensive information on the geography, history, governmental structure, economy, cultural
       diversity, peoples, religion, and culture of Peru" — Provided by publisher.
    Includes bibliographical references and index.
      ISBN-13: 978-0-7614-2068-2
      ISBN-10: 0-7614-2068-1
    1. Peru—Juvenile literature. I. Quek, Lynette. II. Title. III. Series: Cultures of the world (2nd ed.)
    F3408.5.F35 2006
    985—dc22   2005037555

Printed in China

9 8 7 6 5 4 3 2 1

CONTENTS

Schoolgirls in Lima.

A Serrano woman sits on her doorstep spinning wool.

4

INTRODUCTION

PERU IS THE STUFF legends are made of—from the enigmatic "Lost City" of Machu Picchu, to the mysterious Nazca Lines etched on its coastal desert. The land of gold and the cradle of ancient civilizations is also a land of unbridled beauty and mysticism. Peel away its multiple layers, and one will find each face of Peru unique and breathtaking. Whether it is the colonial cities with their Spanish influences, the Andean charm of Cuzco, or the colorful festivals and costumes, one will be struck by Peru's contrasts and surprises. Here, the landscape sweeps from barren deserts to cloud-piercing peaks, vast plateaus, and giant canyons, suddenly plunging into steep valleys of green oases. Although this magnificent country has been through much suffering and turmoil, its people remain vibrantly alive, millions of whom are descendants of the Incas, who still speak the ancient tongue of Quechua and maintain a traditional way of life. All this, combined with the highest biodiversity on the planet, makes Peru unparalleled.

GEOGRAPHY

PERU IS THE THIRD LARGEST South American country, after Brazil and Argentina, and has the fifth largest population. It is a tropical country with its northern tip nearly touching the equator.

Peru has an area of 496,222 square miles (1,285,215 square km)—almost the size of Alaska. Within its borders lies an astonishing range of geographic extremes: from one of the world's driest coasts in the west to the warm and humid Amazon rain forest in the east. The Andes, which form the backbone of the country, are the world's second highest mountain range, and the Colca Canyon is twice as deep as the Grand Canyon. Lake Titicaca is the world's highest navigable lake.

This terrain presents formidable difficulties to its human inhabitants and especially to the farmers, who are at the mercy of a climate that varies from very hot to very cold. It has also been a great obstacle in unifying the nation, dividing the coast's mestizo-Hispanic people, the indigenous Andean people of the highlands, and those of the Amazon Basin. Only recently have roads been built to link remote areas with the rest of the country.

Left: **A desert landscape on the south coast. The Costa, or coastal region, receives less rain than the Sahara in North Africa, and there is very little agricultural activity on it.**

Opposite: **The southwestern face of Nevado Alpamayo is bathed in sunset. It is located in Cordillera Blanca, Ancash, one of Peru's most rugged areas.**

GEOGRAPHIC REGIONS

Peru consists of three main areas: the Costa or western coast along the Pacific Ocean; the Sierra or central Andes highlands and mountains; and the Selva, the rain forests of the Amazon Basin to the east of the Andes.

Made up of deserts, plains, beaches, and valleys, the Costa lies between the Pacific Ocean on the west and the Andes on the east. It varies in width from about 10 to 100 miles (16 to 160 km) and covers just over 10 percent of the country. The Costa has become the most densely populated part of Peru because Lima, the capital, is located there. This small region has attracted nearly half the population of Peru because it offers a higher standard of living, more employment opportunities, and a developed infrastructure.

A large part of Peru is covered by mountains. Because of the high altitude, the air is very thin, and many new visitors are affected by soroche (SAW-roche), or altitude sickness, which produces a feeling of nausea. The local people have adapted to the altitude over generations by developing thick chests and large lungs to efficiently draw the limited oxygen from the air.

Locals relaxing along the city walls of Lima, which is located on the arid Costa, a coastal region that receives very little rain but is shrouded in fog all year long.

Even though the Costa lies beside the ocean, the region is extremely dry and cool, with long stretches of arid plains. The main reason for this is the cold Humbolt current, which flows from the Antarctic, producing sea fogs but little rain. Over 300 species of fish thrive there, turning the area into a fishing paradise and Peru into one of the world's leading producers of fish. To the north is the mineral-rich Sechura Desert.

The Selva (meaning jungle) consists of mountain slopes to the east of the Andes (the area is sometimes called the Montaña) and the part of the Amazon Basin that is in Peru. It occupies nearly two-thirds of the country's territory, and is home to Peru's largest nature reserves. Covered with lush vegetation, the jungle grows more profuse and dense as one ventures eastward. Over 70 percent of the planet's flora and fauna can be found there.

Hundreds of rivers and streams penetrate the jungle, and its inhabitants, including native tribes, settle along the waterways. Rivers are the main highways because roads are quickly destroyed or overgrown. Navigation is hazardous and the water sometimes shallow, but the tribes rely on these rivers as a means to ship local produce, wood, and animals. The area is rich in timber, rubber, coffee, tropical fruit, and medicinal plants. Besides natural gas, 80 percent of Peru's oil reserves are located in this region, and their quantities are sufficient to cover the energy needs of Lima.

The Selva is hot and very humid but teems with wildlife and plants, which flourish probably because the area is so inaccessible.

The imposing Ausangate Mountain overlooks a placid lake. The Andes consist of towering ranges with snowcapped peaks, deep canyons with vertical sides, high, level plains, and active volcanoes in the south.

THE ANDES: BACKBONE OF A CONTINENT

The Andes mountain chain is the longest continuous range in the world, extending more than 4,500 miles (7,240 km) along the western side of South America and passing through many countries from the Isthmus of Panama in the north to Tierra del Fuego in the south. The Peruvian Central Andes, or Sierra, divides the dry coastal region from the tropical Amazon jungle in the east. The Sierra covers a quarter of Peru's surface. The highest mountains in this region are the snowcapped Yerupaja at 21,500 feet (6,550 m) and the Huascarán at 22,205 feet (6,765 m). The Huascarán is also the second highest peak in South America. The average height of the Sierra is around 12,000 feet (3,660 m). The climate of the Sierra is as varied as the landscape. At higher altitudes it can be freezing in any month of the year, but it also gets hotter than at the equator.

There are also many extinct and semiextinct volcanoes in the southern part of the highlands. These cone-shaped volcanoes continue southward down the western side of Lake Titicaca and along the border with Chile and Bolivia. Near the city of Arequipa, the active El Mistí volcano, at 18,000 feet (5,486 m), is the third largest in South America.

The word *andes* is thought to have come from the Incan word *andenes,* which refers to the terraces built by the Incas to level land that was too steep to be irrigated. This terracing system of agriculture enabled large areas of hilly terrain to be cultivated and is still employed in some areas. Although at first they may appear inhospitable to both habitation and farming, over half the world's agricultural specimens are cultivated there.

More people live in the Andes than in any other large highland region in the world. Until recently, a majority of Peruvians lived in the Sierra. Today 36 percent of the population lives there.

The principal reason the Sierra is a population center is because the ancient Incan capital, Cuzco, was located high up in the Andes. Cuzco (meaning navel or center) is said to be the oldest city in South America. During the 13th to 16th centuries, when Incan civilization flourished, it was considered a sacred city and was the heart of the Incan empire.

LAKES AND RIVERS

Lake Titicaca has been a population center since before the Incas. At around 350 miles (560 km) in length and 100 miles (160 km) in width, Titicaca is so large it has waves like the sea. It contains more than 30 islands. Titicaca is Peru's main trade route with Bolivia. It lies at an elevation of 12,500 feet (3,810 m), making it the world's highest navigable body of water.

Other natural trade routes include the many rivers that run through the Selva, some of them tributaries of the Amazon. The Marañón and Ucayali rivers begin 17,200 feet (5,240 m) up in Peru's Andes, merging near Nauta to form the mighty Amazon River, which then gradually plunges down waterfalls to the tropical rain forests that line most of the 2,200 miles (3,540 km) the Amazon travels en route to the Atlantic Ocean.

On September 26, 2005, a major earthquake with a magnitude of 7.5 on the Richter scale shook northern Peru, killing five people and leaving several thousand homeless.

The rise in elevation on the Amazon is so gradual that small ships can reach the town of Iquitos from the Atlantic Ocean.

Plaza San Martín in the
heart of the Peruvian
capital city, Lima.

CITIES

Most of Peru's large cities are located in the coastal area. As Peru's commercial and educational center, Lima and the port at Callao contain over a third of Peru's population. Almost 70 percent of the nation's economic activities are conducted there. It was founded in 1535 by Spanish conquistador Francisco Pizarro, who called it Ciudad de los Reyes, "City of Kings." Other large cities in the Costa include Trujillo, a commercial and industrial center, Chiclayo, and Chimbote.

Most cities in the Andes are small. The largest is Arequipa, a major wool market with about 1 million inhabitants. Located high in the Andes, Cuzco has about 400,000 people and is the ancient Incan capital.

The main town in the Selva is Iquitos, a bustling port city. Located on the banks of the Amazon River, it has about 400,000 inhabitants. Although only 600 miles (965 km) from Lima, Iquitos was so inaccessible before the advent of air travel that to get there from Lima required making a 7,000-mile (11,265-km) journey via the Pacific and through the Panama Canal to the Amazon.

Above: **A three-toed sloth on a tree.**

Opposite: **A piranha is shown baring its teeth.**

FLORA AND FAUNA

Peru is teeming with wildlife. It has over 1,800 species of birds. The waters off the coast hold an abundant and diverse sea life, and along the shore vast numbers of seabirds come to feed on the ocean creatures.

Farther inland, the most famous Peruvian bird is the condor, a rare but beautiful sight in the Andes. It is a large black bird with a white ruff and a wingspan of up to 10 feet (3 m). As a member of the vulture family, the condor usually feeds on dead animals, but it will sometimes kill its prey. It is not, however, a hunter and is unable to grasp or carry prey because its feet are similar to those of a chicken.

In the Andes the equally famous llama was used for centuries as a pack animal before horses and donkeys were introduced. The Spanish brought many new animals to South America. Horses, cows, pigs, chickens, and cattle, none native to Peru, flourished when introduced. The Andes are also home to the puma or mountain lion. The Incas revered the puma as a symbol of power and elegance, but it has suffered recently from indiscriminate hunting. Deer are also common, as is the Andean fox, which frequently raids both sheep herds and garbage cans.

The Selva has many different types of wildlife, including tapirs, jaguars, snakes, monkeys, colorful parrots, alligators, and flesh-eating piranhas. It has been little influenced by humans until recently. Its botanical diversity consists of an average of 500 different tree species per square mile. Tropical rain forests are the oldest continuous terrestrial habitat on earth, so plants have had a much longer time to evolve into different species than in other areas. Although tropical rain forests presently cover less than 2 percent of the earth's surface, they are home to 40 to 50 percent of all plant and animal species on the planet.

LLAMAS

Llamas are native to Peru and have been domesticated since prehistoric times. The Incas used them extensively. Llamas were used to carry burdens, such as food supplies, and for sacrifice in religious ceremonies; their wool and hide were used in clothing and their dung for fuel.

Llamas are useful in the difficult Andean terrain because of their high tolerance for thirst, their endurance, and their ability to subsist on a wide variety of forage. However, when llamas are overloaded or exhausted, they will lie down, hiss, spit, and kick, refusing to move until they are relieved of some of the weight or until they are rested enough to continue the journey.

The llama's head resembles a camel's, with large eyes, a split nose, a harelip, and no upper teeth. Llamas range in color from the common pure white to black, with mixtures of black, brown, and white in between. Their wool is still used for blankets and clothing.

But these animals and, especially, the Amazonian flora are all in danger of possible extinction due to development. Although tropical rain forests have been around for millions of years, they have been on the decline during the last century. This is in direct relation to growth in the human population. At the present rate of destruction, most of the remaining rain forests will be gone within the next 25 years. Although they look lush and healthy, they are extremely fragile, and if cleared for farmland, the soil rarely provides enough nutrients to sustain crops over five years. Conservation has become essentially vital. Peru now has about 5 percent of its land protected by a system of 24 national parks, reserves, and sanctuaries. Conservation groups have also proliferated in recent years.

HISTORY

PERU HAS UNDERGONE MANY CHANGES in its history but has never lost its Incan character. The Incan civilization was the greatest South American empire ever known, even today.

Peru has been ruled by a diverse range of peoples, from the nomadic tribes of the prehistoric period to the city-states from which the Incan empire developed.

The Peruvian republic has been in existence for less than 200 years. For 300 years before that, Peru was under Spanish colonial rule. Spanish domination was followed by self-government, but foreign interests continued to dominate the country. Oligarchy (government by the few), dictatorship, and military coups have plagued its history. Although Peru has found it difficult to shake off authoritarianism, the country has traveled a long way toward establishing democracy.

Above: **A warlike figure decorates a monument, over 3,500 years old, on the Peruvian coast.**

Opposite: **The "lost city" of Machu Picchu rises 8,000 feet (2,440 m) above sea level.**

BEGINNINGS

Peru's first inhabitants were nomadic tribes that probably migrated from Asia and moved into South America over successive generations. Around 5000 B.C. communities began to develop, supported by a growth in agriculture. Corn, gourds, and cotton were cultivated in irrigated fields, and the population began to mushroom.

The Chavíns first united people into a distinct cultural group around 1000 B.C. The Mochica and Nazca cultures dominated Peru from A.D. 200 to 1100. Intertribal warfare meant that no empire could last long or extend very far. These cultures were skilled at producing fine ceramics and elaborate metalwork and at weaving complex designs. The Incan culture, beginning around A.D. 1200, derived much from these tribes' art and architecture while establishing the primacy of the sun cult and the Quechua language.

17

Part of a two–city block long mural by artist Juan Lozavo depicts the Incan civilization.

THE INCAS

The Incas were originally a small tribe, one of many, whose domain did not extend very far from their capital, Cuzco. They were almost constantly at war with neighboring tribes. About A.D. 1200 they began to expand their realm. Their legends do not predate this time.

The Incan empire expanded rapidly with the reign of the ninth emperor, Pachacútec, from 1438 to 1471. This period marked the start of reliable historical records, and differed from earlier times when rulers were considered to be almost mythic. Pachacútec was the most innovative and important of the Incan emperors and is said to have designed and built Cuzco. His first conquest came when his father, Viracocha, placed him in charge of the defense of Cuzco against the neighboring Chancas. Not only did he defend the city, but he also overwhelmingly defeated the Chancas, one of the most powerful confederations in the area. This was the start of a mighty Incan conquest.

From 1463 to 1493 Pachacútec and his son Topa Inca (Emperor Topa) expanded the territory north to the present-day border with Colombia and Ecuador and south as far as Chile. The newly acquired coastline extended

2,500 miles (4,000 km) and encompassed 380,000 square miles (984,200 square km) of territory with a population of around 16 million.

This huge realm was linked by a remarkable road system and was administered through a complex bureaucracy that divided labor and land among the state, the gods, and the *ayllus* (EYE-yoos), or villages. The empire initiated a massive program of agricultural terracing to maximize land use, and also started the construction of palaces and temples.

MACHU PICCHU: REMAINS OF A CIVILIZATION

Yale University archaeologist Hiram Bingham rediscovered the "lost city" of Machu Picchu in 1911. Built on a mountaintop over 500 years ago by the Incas, the ruins are a complex of temples, palaces, and observatories standing 8,000 feet (2,440 m) above sea level. Little is known of the site, for the Incas left no records and the Spanish conquistadors never discovered it. It is believed the city could have been a religious or ceremonial sanctuary, because of the excavation of 173 Incan tombs to date.

Whatever its origins, the site is an astonishing tribute to the architectural skill of the Incas. Situated in a depression high above the Urubamba Valley, these remarkably intact ruins include baths, houses, even cemeteries, all surrounded by terracing on the mountainsides designed to provide food for the residents. Gradually, other ruins in the area are being excavated, which may help unravel the enigma of Machu Picchu.

THE BEGINNING OF THE END

By the end of the 15th century the Incan empire was beginning to suffer from overexpansion. The emperor Huayna Capac created a new Incan city, Quito, the capital of present-day Ecuador. Preferring this city to the traditional Incan center of Cuzco, he ruled the empire from Quito with his favorite son, Atahualpa, and installed his older son, Huáscar, at Cuzco. In the last year of his life he tried to arrange the division of the empire to ensure that Atahualpa retained Quito, but this was rejected by Huáscar, the legitimate heir who was backed by many Cuzco priests and nobles.

With the sudden death of Huayna Capac in 1527, civil war broke out. Atahualpa, backed by his father's army, was more powerful than Huáscar, and in two major victories defeated his half-brother. At the end of the last battle, in 1532, Atahualpa withdrew with his army to the hot baths of Cajamarca in the north of the country. There he soon began hearing strange tales of travelers from afar journeying to meet him.

THE CONQUEST OF THE INCAS

Spanish interest in Peru began with the discovery of the Pacific Ocean in 1513. Tales about the riches inland led Francisco Pizarro, a Spanish soldier, in search of El Dorado, the mythical City of Gold. In 1528 Pizarro, returning from an expedition to the Caribbean, sought the authority of King Charles V of Spain to conquer the new territory. In 1532, with fewer than 180 Spanish adventurers, Pizarro arrived on Peru's northern coast.

Pizarro and his men set out to make contact with Atahualpa, who had just retired victorious from battle and was resting at Cajamarca with an army of 30,000. Pizarro sent a message asking Atahualpa to come and see him. Because Atahualpa was emperor, it was deemed respectful that Pizarro should go to see *him* instead. But Atahualpa made the trip himself, curious to know more about these strange people. He had an entourage of more than 5,000 and did not believe he could possibly be harmed. Although heavily outnumbered, the Spanish had the advantage of surprise. The Spanish also had guns, cannons, horses (which the Incas had never seen before), armor, and chain mail, which made the Incan wooden weapons useless. As a result, most of the Incas were killed, and Atahualpa was taken captive.

Pizarro's capture of Atahualpa and demand for ransom sent the empire into confusion. The wounds had barely healed from the bitter civil war, and now the state was again leaderless. Atahualpa agreed to pay the ransom by filling one room full of gold and another smaller room twice with silver. Incredulous, the Spanish agreed. Within six months a room 22 by 18 feet (7 by 6 m) was filled with gold to a height of 9 feet (3 m). Gold and silver had been ordered from every corner of the empire, enough to make all the men very wealthy, but Pizarro had no intention of keeping his promise. Meanwhile, Atahualpa had been sending secret messages to his nobles in Cuzco. Believing that Huáscar was in league with the Spanish, he ordered Huáscar's death. Pizarro's captains became worried by such maneuvers and, pressuring Pizarro, brought Atahualpa to trial in July 1533, where he was baptized as a Christian and then killed.

In November 1533 Pizarro went to Cuzco, where he appointed a puppet emperor, Manco Inca Yupanqui, to control the populace. Thus began nearly three centuries of colonial rule.

A statue of Francisco Pizarro in Lima. Pizarro and his men repeatedly tricked their way into the confidence of the Incas, only to betray them later.

Manco Inca Yupanqui, a virtual prisoner of the Spanish in Cuzco, escaped in 1536, raised an army, and besieged Spanish strongholds. He was defeated in 1537 and retired to the mountains, where he resorted to guerrilla warfare until his assassination in 1544.

COLONIAL PERU

The consolidation of Spanish control did not run as smoothly as the conquest. Stability was achieved only in 1548, after many internal struggles and much strife among the Spanish conquerors and Incan uprisings that were bloodily suppressed.

The Spanish established a system called the *encomienda* (en-koh-MYEN-dah), whereby allotments of land and natives were given to their men to induce them to stay. This rapidly resulted in serfdom for the native population.

Pizarro founded Lima in 1535, as it made a better transportation center than Cuzco. Wealth was brought to Lima from all over the country and then shipped to Spain. In the various regions of Peru, Spanish *encomenderos* (en-koh-men-DER-ohs), or local agents, exacted taxes from villages. For most of the natives, there was no real difference between their old Incan overlords' exploiting them and the Spanish. The natives had had little chance to identify with the Incan rulers because of the distance they kept from the people, even to the extent of having a separate elite dialect. The Spanish easily stripped the top layer of power away and took its place.

Pizarro was assassinated in 1541, only nine years after the capture of Atahualpa. He was for a time replaced by Diego de Almagro, the son of his fellow conqueror, also named Diego de Almagro. For the next seven years civil war raged among factions of the conquistadors. Worried at this, Spain sent a viceroy, Blasco Nuñez de Vela, in 1544. He was assassinated less than two years later. Spanish government forces were sent and quickly established control in 1548.

Due to the various diseases that the Europeans brought with them, the indigenous population shrank dramatically. In 1520 there were around 32 million natives in the Incan empire; by 1548 there were 5 million.

The cause was mainly smallpox, together with other epidemics, such as the bubonic plague, influenza, and measles. The labor shortage problem was remedied by importing slaves from Africa. Over 1,500 black slaves had arrived in Lima by 1554.

As Spain required more control in Peru than the independent *encomenderos* could provide, the Spanish government divided the country into *corregimientos* (kor-REJ-ee-mee-EN-tos), or units of land, each governed by a royal administrator who limited the power of the *encomenderos*, causing much friction between them.

In 1569 Francisco de Toledo was appointed Peru's fifth viceroy. He reformed the colonial system to increase revenue and also to improve the lot of the natives, who were increasingly being exploited as slaves. One of the ways de Toledo improved native life was by resettling people from remote places, where they were easily manipulated by the *encomenderos*, to cities and towns. Most of his reforms stood for many years but as time went on, became subject to abuses and exploitation.

The 18th century saw the start of uprisings. In Spain the Hapsburgs were replaced by the Bourbons, who tried to stem corruption in the colonies. This led to rebellion between supporters and opponents of the colonialist system in Peru. With the wave of revolutions over Europe and the Americas in the late 18th century, liberal ideas spread and a sense of national identity arose. The newspaper *Mercurio Peruano*, first printed in 1790, began to express concepts of Peruvian nationalism.

A painting of the colonial period depicts the marriage of an Incan princess to a Spanish nobleman.

23

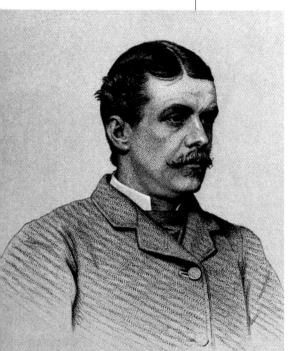

Simón Bolívar, along with José de San Martín, freed Peru from Spanish rule, despite the wishes of most Peruvians. A famous phrase by Bolívar at this time was: *Dos solos no pueden brillar en el mismo firmamento,* or "Two suns cannot shine in the same sky," meaning that only one of them should stay in power.

REBELLION AND REPUBLIC

When Napoleon Bonaparte took control of Spain in 1808, the Spanish colonies were in a state of paralysis. Conflict between those loyal to the deposed Spanish king, Ferdinand VII, and those loyal to the followers of Joseph Bonaparte (Napoleon's brother, whom Napoleon had made king of Spain and Naples), became a source of agitation for revolution. Peru remained more attached to Spain than its Andean neighbors, and it was only with the arrival of outside forces that Peruvian independence became a reality.

Venezuela and Argentina had already declared their independence, and General José de San Martín, one of the great liberators of South America, had in 1817 freed Chile from Spanish rule. San Martín decided it was necessary to liberate Peru, and in 1820 he landed on Peru's southern coast with 5,000 men. On July 28, 1821, San Martín entered Lima and declared all of Peru a republic.

San Martín devised a constitution that gave freedom to the slaves, abolished native servitude, proclaimed the descendants of the Incas to be citizens of Peru, and even banned the insulting term *Indio*. This liberal constitution frightened many of his supporters into a more conservative frame of mind. San Martín returned home to Chile in 1822, leaving his army in Lima. He sought the help of Simón Bolívar, who had already liberated Venezuela, Colombia, and Ecuador, to decisively defeat the royalist armies, offering Bolívar the presidency. Bolívar was president of Peru between 1824 and 1826, and royalist troops were finally defeated at the Battle of Ayacucho in 1824. San Martín's promises to abolish native servitude and to recognize Quechua as an official language were never kept.

A TROUBLED BEGINNING

For two decades there were many internal disputes between the aristocracy and the army. It was only with the presidency of General Ramón Castilla in 1845 that real stability was achieved. Under Castilla, Peru began to seriously exploit its vast and profitable deposits of guano, bird dung used as fertilizer that was found on remote islands. The Castilla administration organized public schools, abolished slavery, and began a railway network to interconnect most of Peru, especially the highlands.

Under Castilla's successors, Peru became increasingly debt-ridden, and its major export, guano, was exhausted. In 1879 Peru went to war with Chile over valuable nitrate deposits in Peru and Bolivia. The four-year War of the Pacific ended with Peru's loss of the nitrate fields to Chile. Peru also lost ownership of much of its infrastructure and natural resources to foreigners.

In the 40 years after independence from Spain, the presidency changed hands 35 times, and the country generated at least 15 different constitutions. In this period only four of the presidents were constitutionally chosen, and the vast majority were military figures.

The ineffectiveness of the presidents who came after Castilla provoked many revolts. Nicolás de Piérola, after heading unsuccessful revolts in 1874 and 1877, finally overthrew the president in 1895. During his administration Peru adopted the gold standard, and civil marriages were legalized. He is shown entering Lima on March 17, 1895, in this picture.

TWENTIETH CENTURY

Peru entered the 20th century with some stability but was governed by rich businessmen and landowners. With the presidency of Augusto Leguía y Salcedo (1908–12 and 1919–30), the country rapidly expanded its mineral and agricultural industries and developed its oil reserves. Lima was modernized with beautiful plazas and parks, but the rest of the country remained unchanged.

In 1963 Peru returned to civilian rule with Fernando Belaúnde Terry as president. The armed forces overthrew Belaúnde in the coup of 1968. They expanded the role of the state, nationalized several industries and embarked on agrarian reform. Plantations were turned into peasant cooperatives, while foreign companies and banks were nationalized. These initiatives failed miserably, and the economy remained problematic in the years ahead.

Former President Fernando Belaúnde Terry's second term was marked by economic problems and the rise of the terrorist group Sendero Luminoso.

After 12 years of military rule, free elections were held and Belaúnde was reelected president in 1980. The emergence of *Sendero Luminoso* (sen-DER-oh loo-mee-NOH-soh) or "Shining Path" gave rise to terrorist attacks by the Maoist group, which resulted in 69,280 deaths from 1980 to 2000. In 1985 Alan García Pérez from the APRA (Alianza Popular Revolucionaria Americana) won the elections, but with the rise of terrorism, there seemed to be no resolution to Peru's divisions.

FUJIMORI'S ADMINISTRATION

In 1990 political novice Alberto Fujimori, of East Asian descent, defeated noted novelist Mario Vargas Llosa for the presidency. Fujimori's radical economic reforms included the privatization of state-owned companies.

Fujimori staged a military coup in April 1992, suspended Congress, and declared a state of emergency to combat terrorism. September's capture of Shining Path's leader, Abimael Guzmán, diminished the rebels' grip on Peru, but the movement continued to live on.

Accusations of a tainted reelection and serious rioting eventually forced the disgraced president to resign in November 2000. He fled to Japan, and was shielded from extradition by Japanese citizenship, which was granted after his arrival. Fujimori was arrested in Chile in November 2005 while en route to Peru to join the 2006 presidential elections. The Toledo administration intends to make Fujimori face charges of corruption and human rights abuse when he is extradited to Peru.

RECENT HISTORY

Peru's recent history of turmoil includes over two decades of political mayhem and corruption, terrorism and economic disarray. In July 2001 the election of economist Alejandro Toledo, Peru's first native president, created much hope for change. However, his presidency has been plagued by fears of a Shining Path reprise, corruption allegations, a drug scandal, and rumors of his having fathered a daughter from an extramarital affair.

Although Peru has had the fastest-growing economy in Latin America—four years of growth averaging 4.8 percent each year—54 percent of the population still lives in poverty. Unemployment hit 9.3 percent in 2005. Public dissatisfaction arises from Peru's uneven distribution of wealth. Resources are concentrated in Lima and other major cities, while conditions in the rural and provincial areas continue to worsen. Rising discontent led to massive strikes and demonstrations throughout 2003 and 2004.

President Alejandro Toledo is Peru's first president of native origin but his term has been mired in political crisis.

27

GOVERNMENT

PERU'S CURRENT CONSTITUTION, approved by referendum on October 31, 1993, is Peru's fifth in the 20th century. Under this constitution Peru is a constitutional republic with independent executive, legislative, and judicial branches of government. The constitution was amended in 2000 to prohibit the president from seeking reelection for a second consecutive 5-year term.

Voting is mandatory for citizens 18 to 70 years of age, except for those in the military and National Police. A candidate must gain 50 percent of the vote to be directly elected as president. If none of the candidates can garner half the votes, a second round of voting will be conducted between the two strongest contenders. Alejandro Toledo was inaugurated as president in July 2001, and governed until July 28, 2006. He was succeeded by Alan Garcia, who won the second round of the 2006 presidential elections with a slender 52.5 percent of votes over his rival, Ollanta Humala.

Above: **Alan García Pérez narrowly won the 2006 presidential elections. He was formerly president from 1985 to 1990, and his policies led to a period of soaring inflation in the late 1980s.**

Opposite: **Peruvian troops in armored vehicles in Barranca after President Toeldo imposed a 30-day emergency in 2003.**

THE EXECUTIVE

The president is the chief of state, head of government, and supreme chief of the armed forces and National Police. He oversees national defense and has the power to enforce laws, declare war and sign peace treaties, and order emergency decrees, among other responsibilities.

The first and second vice presidents are elected for the same term but have no constitutional functions unless the president cannot carry out his duties. Headed by the prime minister, the 15-member Council of Ministers (cabinet) approves legislative decrees and bills sent to Congress.

A guard outside a government building in Lima.

THE LEGISLATURE

The legislative branch is a unicameral Congress, with 120 members elected at the same time as the president, also for a five-year term. Besides passing laws and amending or repealing existing laws, Congress is responsible for approving the budget, loans, and international treaties. The president can reject legislation that the executive branch does not approve. Congress can also appoint commissions to conduct investigations of public interest.

Over time, reforms have significantly improved decentralization and strengthened institutional checks and balances. In 2000 Congress dissolved the National Intelligence Service, abolished the state of emergency, and reinstated constitutional guarantees. In 2001 it recognized the jurisdiction of the Inter-American Court of Human Rights, and a 1995 amnesty that favored the military was lifted.

THE LEGAL SYSTEM

The 1993 constitution provided for a Supreme Court of Justice, superior courts, specialized and mixed courts, justices of the peace, and lawyers. There is one Supreme Court for the entire country, while there is a Superior Court in each judicial district. Judges (except for justices of the peace, who are elected) are appointed and removed by the National Justice Council.

The 16-member Supreme Court in Lima is the highest court in the land. Superior courts sit in regional capitals and hear appeals from lower courts. Courts in the provincial capitals are divided into civil, penal, and special chambers, and have jurisdiction over all serious crime. Justices of the peace are the lowest courts and have jurisdiction over petty crime and minor civil matters. These courts are found in most local towns.

The National Elections Board establishes voting laws, registers parties and their candidates, and supervises elections, which it has the power to void if there are irregularities. In 1996 the Office of the Human Rights Ombudsman was formed to protect the people's constitutional rights and to supervise the duties of the State and its public services.

This presidential election slogan is painted on a wall in Ollantaytambo.

The military distributing grain to the poor.

REGIONAL AND LOCAL GOVERNMENT

The administration of Peru has traditionally been very centralized, and only recently have regional governments been given powers independent of the national government in Lima. Peru is divided into 25 administrative regions, including the constitutional province of Callao. All regions are further divided into provinces and subdivided into districts. There are 180 provinces and 1,747 districts. The city of Lima and greater Lima, however, do not belong to any particular region, and are referred to as Lima Metropolitana (Metropolitan Lima).

Peruvians elected their own regional presidents and other local authorities in 2002. Under the Decentralization Framework Act, decision-making powers, budget, and taxation authority will be transferred to the 25 regional governments over a 10-year period. They will manage their own infrastructure, revenues, and services, among other responsibilities. This is meant to devolve power to provincial governments and improve public access to services. Financial aid programs will fund the process.

RECENT EVENTS

Fujimori's removal in 2000 paved the way for democracy and Peru's reconciliation process. In 2001 the government set up the Truth and Reconciliation Commission (CVR) to investigate the political killings that devastated Peru from 1980 to 2000. During this period the civil war waged by Shining Path guerrillas and the Túpac Amaru Revolutionary Movement (MRTA) in Peru's remote regions wiped out the indigenous communities that lived there.

Former President Alberto Fujimori was forced into exile in Japan after a series of political scandals. He was arrested in Chile in 2005, pending extradition charges.

After 17,000 testimonies, the commission released its final report in August 2003, concluding that 69,280 Peruvians had been killed or went missing in the violence on both sides. Over 11,500 cases of crimes against humanity were documented, including those of torture, massacre, rape, slavery, and kidnapping. The Shining Path was responsible for 54 percent of the deaths, the Peruvian armed forces for 28 percent. The rest were attributed to civilian defense groups and the MRTA.

The majority of the victims belonged to the most marginalized groups, namely Quechua-speaking indigenous people, peasants, farmers, and rural dwellers. Some 600,000 inhabitants were displaced from their homes. Ethnic discrimination was one of the reasons why the suffering and fatalities of these defenseless civilians had gone unnoticed for 20 years.

Some 378 former military and police officers have been charged for gross human rights violations. The government has offered 2,845 million soles ($845 million) in compensation to the victims and their families. It will provide education grants to war orphans and funding for violence-affected areas. In May 2004, a new law recognized the special rights and needs of the displaced, including their eligibility for compensation.

ECONOMY

THERE IS AN OLD FRENCH EXPRESSION, "to be as rich as Peru," which suggests how wealthy Peru was once considered. Then the main exports were gold and silver. Present-day Peru is still a land of extremely rich natural resources, but also one of much poverty, unemployment, and underemployment. The current Peruvian economy is one of the strongest in Latin America.

When Alberto Fujimori was president from 1990 to 2000, he privatized hundreds of state-owned industries, reducing inflation and increasing growth in the process. Driven by foreign investment, the economy was on the upswing from 1994 through 1997, but stagnated from 1998 through 2001. Since President Alejandro Toledo took over in 2001, Peru's economy has grown from strength to strength, with gross domestic product (GDP) rates—the total monetary value of all goods and services produced in a country— increasing every year, recording an all-time high of 6.6 percent in 2005.

Left: **A sawmill in Pucallpa.**

Opposite: **Vendors selling fresh vegetables at a market in Peru.**

Peru's robust growth has not led to greater job opportunities, and 54 percent of the population remains mired in poverty. This is partly because of the reliance on industries such as mining, which typically have low turnover rates.

FACTS AND FIGURES

In 2005 Peru had a GDP of $78.2 billion. The average GDP per capita for that year was $2,798. Recent economic expansion has been fueled by construction, mining, manufacturing, fishing, investment, domestic demand, and exports. Inflation fell from 3.5 percent in 2004 to 2.1 percent in 2005. The fiscal deficit also fell from 1.4 percent of the GDP in 2004 to around 1 percent in 2005. Although Peru is not heavily industrialized, its service sector contributes 65 percent to the GDP. Exports valued at $11.4 billion in 2004 included gold, copper, fish products, petroleum, zinc, textiles, asparagus, and coffee. Major imports include machinery, vehicles, steel, and processed food. Analysts predict the GDP may grow further as a result of surging demand for Peruvian exports, increased private investments, and higher consumption levels.

A textile factory in the city of Arequipa.

OIL AND ENERGY

Peru began exporting oil in the late 19th century when oil fields were first developed on the north coast. New fields were discovered in the Amazon region, and when the petroleum industry was nationalized in 1968 as Petroperu (privatized in 1993), these new fields began to be developed. A billion-dollar pipeline was completed in 1976 to pipe oil from the jungle over the Andes to the coast. Oil reserves, however, have been in steady decline since the 1980s. An average of 95,500 barrels per day were produced in 2004, compared with 195,000 in 1982.

Most of Peru's energy needs are satisfied by oil, while the balance are met by electricity and natural gas. In August 2004 the Camisea natural gas project began its operations. Composed of several natural gas fields located in the Urubamba Valley of the Peruvian Amazon, Camisea fuels an electricity generator and six industrial plants in Lima. The gas there is equivalent to 2.4 million barrels of oil, about seven times the size of Peru's oil reserves. It provides for domestic consumption and is expected to transform Peru into a net energy exporter.

An oil pump on the Peruvian coast. Production of oil has diminished over the past few years, but Peru is protected from recession as it enjoys a wealth of other natural resources, including natural gas and copper.

Around 88 percent of all electricity in Peru is generated at hydroelectric plants. Peru's water resources have the potential to create 30 times that amount!

Cotton pickers working on a plantation near Ica. The most important export crops are cotton, coffee, and sugarcane. Potatoes, rice, plantains, as well as corn are also produced in great quantities but are grown mainly for domestic consumption.

The principal livestock in Peru are sheep, cattle, pigs, and goats. The llama is used as a pack animal in the mountains.

AGRICULTURE

The agricultural sector accounts for 9 percent of Peru's GDP. Climatic conditions in the countryside make possible the cultivation of different crops throughout the year, including sugarcane, potato, rice, corn, asparagus, tomato, and jojoba, which yields a valuable wax used in cosmetics. It also has a wide variety of fruit and medicinal plants such as cat's claw and maca. Almost 80 percent of agricultural workers own small plots of land or are peasants who communally share pasture. Most farmers produce mainly for themselves.

Before 1968 most land was divided into large estates that were owned by a small minority. The 1969 agrarian reform transformed the estates into peasant cooperatives. About 24 million acres (10 million ha) of agricultural land were expropriated, and 400,000 families benefited. In the 1980s the land was divided into small plots, placing more stress on individual enterprise. Overall, this policy was not successful, because the land usually provided insufficient yields to sustain small farms. Moreover, the farmers often lacked capital and experience to sell their produce.

Agricultural production in Peru is commonly affected by unpredictable weather, limited arable land, poor organization, and lack of transportation. Poor soil also plays a part, and the diminishing supply of guano (traditionally used as fertilizer) has resulted in increasing reliance on chemical fertilizers, which are less effective, more environmentally destructive, and expensive. For these reasons, staple foods often have to be imported. Peru's most infamous crop is the coca leaf, which is refined to make cocaine.

WHITE GOLD

To the Incas, coca was known as the divine plant. Because coca was used in religious festivals and rites to induce ecstasies and visions, it was regarded as a sacred plant. Coca continued to be accepted after the conquest—even the Spanish clergy were enthusiastic about it. Chewing coca leaves suppresses hunger, thirst, and exhaustion, allowing people to do more work than normal, supposedly double their ordinary workload. The Spanish conquistadors found it vital in manipulating the natives, who were given large quantities of the leaves and literally worked to death in the silver and gold mines. Before the Spanish conquest, coca leaves *(below)* were used only occasionally, to stave off hunger caused by a shortage of food or to lighten the burden of work, and this continues today.

In the 19th century coca and its more potent derivative, cocaine, were thought to be good for health, especially when made into a tonic or wine. This quickly changed as cocaine became recognized as a powerful, addictive, and deadly drug. In Peru cocaine is illegal, but coca leaves are not. In 2004 Peru's coca crops covered about 124,294 acres (50,300 ha)—approximately the same area of land under coca cultivation in 1998.

Past attempts to decrease or destroy the cocaine trade have met with failure. Buying up the crop or substituting different crops have been almost impossible strategies because of the rapid increase in land devoted to coca growing. No other crop is anywhere nearly as profitable as coca. Coca is three times more profitable than cocoa and almost 40 times more profitable than corn.

As the temptation of a much higher income is often difficult to resist, peasants will only abandon coca cultivation if legitimate means to earn a stable livelihood are available. The United Nations Office on Drugs and Crime (UNODC) has stepped up its alternative livelihood programs across the Andean region. UNODC data indicate that farmers involved in its program, such as those in palm oil production, earn three times more than their counterparts who are involved in coca cultivation.

In recent years the drug trade has become inextricably linked with terrorism. Sendero Luminoso (Shining Path) terrorists have forced a partnership on the peasants, protecting growers against government interference in exchange for some of the profits. In an attempt to get rid of Sendero, the military has tried to ally itself with the coca growers. This means tolerating the growers and their crops while the fight against Sendero Luminoso continues.

A fish meal plant located near Lima.

FISHING

Peru's fishing industry rapidly expanded to become the world's largest in 1970. The main fish was the Peruvian anchovy, which was converted into fish meal and oil for export. In 1994 Peru became the world's second fishing nation after China, with a total catch of 11.6 million tons. It is also the world's leading fish meal producer, accounting for 60 percent of the world's exports in 2001. The industry, however, took a beating in 1998, when exports plunged as a result of El Niño's rampage.

MINING

Although mining employs only 0.9 percent of the population, it provides 48.6 percent of foreign earnings, 10 percent of which come from Yanacocha, the world's most profitable gold mine. Other major deposits are silver, copper, lead, and zinc. Peru holds 16 percent of the world's silver reserves and is a leader in silver production. It has 15 percent of the world's copper reserves and is the fifth largest producer of copper and tin. It also contains 7 percent of the total zinc found on earth, and is the fourth biggest in zinc and lead production.

Guano-covered cliffs on Ballestas Island. Guano was once Peru's most important export. Between 1840 and 1880, Peru exported 11 million tons of it.

EXPORTS

Prior to the 20th century Peru's main exports were guano and gold. Now almost a quarter of Peru's income comes from exporting raw materials. The country produces a variety of exports and does not depend on one particular item for income. In 2004 Peruvian mineral exports brought in $6.77 billion, an increase of 44 percent from 2003. Along with Bolivia, Colombia, and Ecuador, Peru benefits greatly from the Andean Trade Promotion and Drug Eradication Act, which provides duty-free access to the United States for 6,300 products. Since its 2002 initiation, two-way trade between the United States and the Andean countries has doubled.

TOURISM

Peru is an attractive South American destination for tourists. Peruvians are hospitable, and the country offers much to the tourist in terms of natural beauty, historical sites, and cultural variety. The tourism industry is an important and fast-growing economic sector but has suffered because of crime, attacks on tourists, and the ever-present terrorist threat. Even so, in a good year the tourist industry can make over $1 billion.

ENVIRONMENT

PERU IS AMONG THE WORLD'S TOP FIVE most ecologically and biologically diverse countries. Blessed with a mosaic of landscapes—coastal deserts, Andean highlands, and Amazonian forests—each with its own climate, Peru sustains an astonishing array of ecosystems, plant species, and wildlife. Over 80 percent of the earth's ecological zones can be found here.

Human activities, however, continue to threaten Peru's environment. The country's environmental woes are exacerbated, or made worse, by a lack of governance and regulation. Its natural resources have long been recognized and overexploited. As a result, more than 5.9 million acres (2.4 million ha) of land have been degraded.

Deforestation, uncontrolled logging, pollution, dumping of mining wastes, overfishing, overgrazing, desertification, and extensive coca cultivation are just some of Peru's major environmental concerns.

DEFORESTATION

According to 2005 figures from the United Nations's Food and Agriculture Organization, over 169 million acres (68 million ha) or 53.7 percent of Peru's territory is covered in natural-growth forest. This ranks Peru as the country with the fourth largest tropical forest area in the world.

About 70 percent of Peru's forests are found in the Amazon Basin—one of the oldest, largest, richest, and most complex ecosystems on earth. Located in the country's eastern regions, the rain forest provides a habitat for an immense range of organisms and acts as a watershed for the planet's aquatic systems. More importantly, it serves as a regulator of the earth's climate.

Above: **Fishing on the Amazon River.**

Opposite: **The Huascarán National Park is located within the Andes's Cordillera Blanca, the world's highest tropical mountain chain.**

At current deforestation rates, scientists estimate nearly all tropical rain forest ecosystems will be destroyed by the year 2030.

—Rainforest Action Network

Unfortunately, much of the Amazon Basin is under threat. Between 2000 and 2005 Peru lost about 554,998 acres (224,600 ha) of primary forest per year. This is largely attributed to agricultural, logging, and farming activities. Using the slash-and-burn technique, dense forests are cleared for cattle grazing and crop cultivation, while roads are built for logging. Overgrazing by livestock loosens the soil and leads to soil erosion. Even the mighty cloud forests in the Andes have been deforested by unsustainable potato farming and dairy production.

A deforested plot can be burned just twice before it becomes infertile. Studies have shown that leaving the rain forests intact, with their wealth of latex, nuts, and medicinal plants, has far greater economic value than destroying them for unsustainable short-term interests. When these natural habitats are destroyed, indigenous people lose their land, livelihood, and culture, and plant and animal species become extinct.

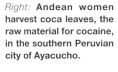

Right: **Andean women harvest coca leaves, the raw material for cocaine, in the southern Peruvian city of Ayacucho.**

Opposite: **Illegal and legal logging have drastically reduced the amount of timber in the Peruvian Amazon.**

Another leading cause of deforestation is Peru's most controversial export—coca. Severe poverty drives peasant farmers to cultivate coca for the production of cocaine. Large areas on the Andean hillsides are destroyed for illegal plantations, which supply about two-thirds of the world's cocaine. As coca crops tend to rob the land of nutrients and cause soil erosion, replacement crops cannot be grown.

In addition, farmers spray pesticides on the plants, contaminating the soil and nearby waterways. Toxic chemicals are also widely used by local authorities to eradicate the illegal crop.

LOGGING

Throughout the Amazon Basin, commercial loggers, illegal and legal, are plundering the forests in search of prized timber such as mahogany and cedar. According to the Research Institute of the Peruvian Amazon, as much as 95 percent of the endangered mahogany from Peru is logged illegally. Mahogany's value—a single tree is worth around $300,000 in the international market—attracts prospectors who bulldoze deep into the forests and even into national parks and nature reserves.

Logging is also impacting indigenous people who depend on the forest for survival. Given that timber exports have been rising 25 percent per year over the past five years, it is estimated that Peruvian mahogany could become extinct by as early as 2010 to 2015.

AIR, WATER, AND LAND POLLUTION

It is estimated that 60 percent of all solid waste in Lima is thrown into makeshift dumps, nearby rivers and oceans, or used in illegal livestock operations. A startling 40 percent of the entire population does not have access to waste disposal facilities; hence, waste is often dumped or burned. Industrial and household wastes, including those from fish meal production, contaminate the coastal rivers and lakes, while waterways in the Amazon Basin are sterile due to sludge deposits from oil extractions.

Mines dump cyanide, mining waste, and mercury into the streams, while smelter emissions pollute the air, especially in the highlands. Almost 15 million gallons (57 million l) of liquid waste from coca processing have been discarded into the waters and on land. Heavy metal has been found in virtually every sediment that was analyzed along the coast, as well as in marine life.

The mountain tapir is one of many species facing extinction due to illegal wildlife trading.

ENDANGERED SPECIES

The spectacled bear, giant river otter, marine turtle, mountain tapir, jaguar, and Humboldt penguin are just some examples of the Peruvian wildlife species that are being threatened.

In 2002 Earth Trends listed 269 plant species, 49 mammals, 76 breeding birds, and six reptiles that are endangered in Peru. Of these, 10 animal species are classified as critically endangered, 28 species as endangered, and 99 species are considered vulnerable by CITES (Convention on International Trade in Endangered Species of Wild Fauna and Flora).

The Paracas National Park in Pisco is a famous UNESCO World Heritage Natural Site.

Illegal trade in wildlife is a multibillion-dollar business. Exotic animals are captured alive and sold as pets or for research. Some are killed for their body parts and sold as food, clothing, accessories, and medicine. Others, like primates and lizards, are raised in captivity for the international market. Wild plants are commonly traded for use in botanical and pharmaceutical products. For many of these endangered plants and animals, such trade can lead to their extinction and is, therefore, a great threat to the ecological system and global biodiversity.

PROTECTED AREAS

Peru has set aside several national parks and reserves for conservation. These cover more than 10 percent of Peru's land, and include the Manú Biosphere Reserve, the Tambopata-Candamo Reserve Zone, and the Pacaya-Samiria National Reserve, which are three of the largest protected rain forest areas in the world. UNESCO has designated the Huascarán National Park (in Huaráz), Manú National Park (in Madre de Dios), and

A pair of scarlet macaws enjoy the view overlooking the Tambopata River in Manú National Park.

Río Abiseo National Park (in San Martín) as World Heritage Sites.

Home to the spectacled bear and the Andean condor, Huascarán National Park's jaw-dropping ravines, glacial lakes, and the world's highest tropical mountain peak, Mount Huascarán, make it a site of spectacular beauty. The massive Manú National Park is equally impressive—the rare giant otter, giant armadillo, and jaguar seek refuge there. Rain forests with characteristics that are unique to the Andes are protected in the Río Abiseo National Park. The yellow-tailed woolly monkey is also endemic, or native, to the area.

ECO GROUPS

An increasing number of environmental organizations and movements now exist in Peru to protect the environment and preserve the indigenous people's culture and rights. INRENA, the National Institute of Natural Resources, enforces logging regulations and reseeds Peru's share of the Amazon forest. A handful of international and local conservation groups, such as ProNaturaleza, Conservation International, and the Rainforest Action Network are active, working on reforestation and sustainable forestry projects in Peru.

The ACEER Foundation (Amazon Center for Environmental Education and Research) is a unique research center that aims to improve local awareness of the environment. Located within a 24,711-acre (10,000-ha) reserve at Tambopata, it offers education and research programs, conducts nature tours, a field lab, demonstration gardens, interpreted trails, and a nature interpretation center for scientists and students.

CONSERVATION LAWS AND TREATIES

Recent environmental laws in Peru provide for more controlled forms of sustainable resource use, in place of older policies that encouraged aggressive industrial development in the Amazon Basin. Peru has ratified the Antarctic-Environmental Protocol and the Antarctic Treaty in April 1981, and is a member of CITES. It has also signed some of the most important international conservation agreements such as the Convention on Biodiversity, the Convention to Combat Desertification, and the Conservation of Migratory Species of Wild Animals. Others concern the wetlands, climate change, the world's cultural and natural heritage, hazardous wastes, nuclear tests, the ozone layer, ship pollution, and timber logging. Regionally, Peru participates in several treaties on sustainable land use in the Amazon Basin.

Peru has approximately 5,000 laws and regulations pertaining to environmental protection and resource conservation. However, most of these are not enforced or are only partially implemented. Some of the problems lie with the institutional weakness of environmental agencies (limited political power, scant human and economic resources); unregulated industries that continue to degrade the environment; weak deterrence and punishment mechanisms; and the lack of a long-term national development strategy for the environment.

PERUVIANS

PERU IS HOME TO extremely varied groups of people. Intermarriage among the groups over the centuries has made racial classification difficult, because many distinctions are largely a matter of choice. Peruvians define people of mixed Spanish and native ancestry as either mestizo (mes-TEE-zoh) or *cholo* (CHOH-loh). *Cholos* are native people who are attempting to cross over into white society, whereas mestizos are already socially established.

Such vague distinctions show how confusing Peru's ethnic groupings are. A person may consider himself mestizo, while people around him think he is a *cholo*. These distinctions are not so much racially as culturally defined. Officially Peru's ethnic mix is: European 15 percent, mestizos 37 percent, indigenous 45 percent, and African, Japanese, Chinese, and others 3 percent.

Above: **Though Peru is a predominantly Roman Catholic country, it has a low population growth rate of only 1.4 percent, as many women of childbearing age use contraception.**

Opposite: **An indigenous girl from one of the many villages located along the Amazon River smiles for the camera.**

POPULATION FACTS AND FIGURES

Peru's population is approximately 28 million. About 75 percent of Peruvians live in urban areas, a figure that reflects increased migration to the cities in the last two decades.

A Peruvian's average life expectancy is 69 years. Although the country is strongly Roman Catholic, a religion that forbids artificial birth control, the annual growth rate is only 1.4 percent. Over 50 percent of married women of childbearing age use contraception but families are often larger than North American families, with four to seven children per household.

A fair Peruvian, as shown above, is not necessarily elite, because the term refers to a class based on wealth and position, as well as one's ancestry.

SOCIAL CLASSES

The Spanish conquerors established a class system based on race, one in which the white upper class ruled the lower class of natives. In the 20th century a middle class of mestizos developed. Today most people remain in the social class they were born into; education is the main avenue for advancement.

The coastal and Sierra regions have quite different elite, middle, and lower classes, the urbanization of the coast having produced totally different social conditions from the rural Sierra.

THE ELITE The coastal elite, numbering only a small percentage of the total population, is composed of people from various prestigious backgrounds: members of the agricultural aristocracy, successful immigrants or their children, and the Peruvian representatives of foreign businesses. Descendants from the old Spanish families form one of the largest segments of the elite.

The wealth of the elites comes from banking, finance, marketing, land ownership, or industry. Until the military coup of 1968, 44 families dominated Peruvian affairs in nearly every sphere. This small number owned a substantial amount of the land, estimated at more than 70 percent of the country.

The military dictatorship, which was mainly middle-class and mestizo, stripped these families of some of their wealth, but the redistribution still went mainly to the top 25 percent of the population. Most of the elite live in Lima and Callao, less often in Trujillo and Arequipa. Those who live in the Sierra have declined in significance as their power in local government and agriculture has been eroded. Estates were divided by inheritance laws and families became less influential until, in 1969, nearly all land holdings were taken from them.

One of the main ways the elite on the coast retained their privileges was to diversify into business and finance instead of relying on their private estates for wealth. They have also used kinship bonds to incorporate the newly rich into their society and strengthen ties with other families.

THE MIDDLE CLASS Only around 15 to 17 percent of Peruvians belong to the middle class. Like the elite, the middle class is mainly urban, educated, and speaks Spanish. Peru's middle class looks to the elite for its values. It is not surprising that over half the middle class is employed by the government.

A Peruvian family in front of their house. Middle-class occupations include doctors, teachers, professors, lawyers, small business persons, shop owners, and the military, as well as government employees.

The middle class in the Sierra is wholly dependent on cheap native labor and is itself in the employ of the elite, looking after their estates and filling local government and administrative posts.

In postwar Peru (since 1945) and particularly during the period of military dictatorship, a new middle class developed. This new group relied on its own expertise rather than on the elite for employment. Modernization in the 1970s created middle-class prosperity, but hyperinflation in the 1980s wiped out much of their savings.

With recent political events and the elites' diminishing power, the middle class is now taking the lead in the creation of a new and modern Peru.

IMMIGRANTS

Until independence, Peru was not open to immigration, and the only foreign arrivals were the few African slaves imported to work on plantations. Foreigners began arriving in Peru in the 1830s. Compared with Brazil or Argentina, immigration was not large scale and was usually work related. Chinese immigrants came between 1850 and 1875 to work on the railroads and guano deposits. (The picture shows a lion dance in Lima's Chinatown.) Many Japanese arrived in Peru in the early 20th century, and today around 80,000 people of Japanese descent live there. In the business community, British and North Americans are the biggest groups, but there is also a small number of Europeans and Arabs. The neighboring countries of Colombia, Chile, Bolivia, and Ecuador have contributed around 20,000 new residents.

A slum in Lima.

THE LOWER CLASS The lower class is highly diverse, including nearly 80 percent of the population. It includes the unemployed, laborers, small farmers, small shopkeepers, itinerant traders, artisans, servants, and enlisted military personnel.

Because of this diversity, the lower class has great difficulty in forming an organized front or creating a union powerful enough to take on the bosses. Farm laborers have little in common with small farm owners. Even highly skilled union members find it more advantageous to make alliances with the middle-class professional unions.

The family is one of the most important aspects of life for the lower class. Marriages in the Sierra are more stable than those in the coastal areas. Parental authority is also more evident and respected in the Sierra.

Families gather and organize entertainment, fiestas, soccer games, and dances that the whole community enjoys. Associations springing from family ties and affiliations also try to organize political and economic activities, pressuring politicians and local landowners for support or change.

NATIVE PEOPLES

The native peoples can be subdivided into two groups, those from the Andes Sierra region and those from the Selva.

THE ANDEAN NATIVES The Aymará and the Quechua populate central and southern Andes. The Quechua live mainly in the Sierra departments of Ancash, Ayacucho, and Cuzco. Several other departments, or administrative subdivisions, that have a high proportion of Quechua speakers are Junín, Huánuco, Huancavelica, and Apurímac. The Aymará are found mainly in Puno, although many have migrated to the southern departments of Arequipa, Moquegua, and Tacna. Because of steady migration in the 20th century, substantial numbers of both native groups now live in the cities, especially Lima.

The Aymará and Quechua live side by side, although there is little intermarriage between them. The Aymará are likely to speak Spanish and Quechua; the Quechua, Spanish. They both hold stereotyped views of

The faces of these Andean men recall the features of the Incas.

Cholos provide an important link between the natives and national institutions, enabling them to influence the national, political, and social agendas.

A native woman from Tinqui with her daughter. In a 1970s reform, natives were renamed peasants instead of Indians, as the term Indian was considered insulting. At one stage, it was even illegal to use the word Indian in reference to the Aymará or Quechua peoples.

each other: the Aymará consider the Quechua old-fashioned, uneducated, and lazy, whereas the Quechua think the Aymará are stubborn, argumentative, and money-minded.

Mestizos and whites make no distinction when it comes to the natives: they look down on the natives. A popular Sierra saying goes, "The Indian is the animal closest to man." The native is almost universally despised by Peruvians, who hold them to be inferior, drunken, superstitious, dirty, lazy, and addicted to coca. Despite the military regime's reforms in the 1970s, the natives are still dislocated from the rest of the country's people. Some native families who have risen socially go to great lengths to mask their native origins.

There is, however, a great deal of social mobility between the natives and mestizos. Natives who adopt Spanish as their main language, don Western rather than traditional clothing, and take up a mestizo occupation are called *cholos*, an insulting term that suggests the person is trying to rise above his or her proper social place.

THE AMAZON NATIVES A much more diverse collection of tribes lives east of the Andes in the Amazon Basin. Although there are only around 200,000 natives in the Peruvian Amazon, they belong to 53 different ethnic groups, speaking 12 main languages and many varied dialects. Some tribes have only a handful of members still living, whereas others, like the Jívaro with 8,000 members and the Campa with 21,000, are doing very well.

A Jívaro man poses for the camera. Like most tribes, the Jívaro use hallucinogenic drugs to see into the supernatural world and give them the power to cure or bewitch other people.

The Amazonian peoples have a fierce and warlike reputation. The Incas, although powerful builders of an empire, could not subdue them, and there are many legends of hordes of Amazons repeatedly sacking Cuzco. Generally, the Incas left these people alone, except to trade with them in cloth, bronze, axes, exotic fruits, and wood. When the Spanish arrived, they, too, were confronted with various tribes who would not accept their authority. Expeditions into the jungle ended in Spanish annihilation.

One of the fiercest and most interesting Amazon tribes thriving today is the Jívaro, who have resisted attempts to conquer them. They still live in their tropical forest homeland to the east of the Andes. The Jívaro fish and hunt with blowguns and poison darts. They keep domestic animals, gather berries and roots from the forest, and plant banana trees and manioc, a root vegetable. On small handlooms men weave cloth into kiltlike skirts, which are worn by both men and women. Chiefs and shamans wear feathers denoting their status. Each small white bone worn on the left shoulder of a warrior represents a man he has killed. Women usually wear robes pinned on one shoulder, but some people wear ponchos.

Above: **A house in the Selva. The homes of the Campa are often without walls and consist of a palm-thatched roof supported by poles.**

Opposite: **A Yaguas man with his blowpipe.**

Family life revolves around the house, which can hold 30 to 40 relatives. Polygamy is common because of the shortage of men due to warfare, mostly waged between different Jívaro communities.

The Campa, to the east of the Andes, are similar to the Jívaro in their not having been conquered by either the Incas or the Spanish. They are also alike in repulsing missionaries, especially those who seek to impose monogamy. By 1800 the Campa were left in peace. Although as hostile and resistant to invasion as the Jívaro, they have had to put up with settlers occupying their land.

Clothing is made from jungle materials—bark cloth is reddened with dye and worn like a robe. Men and boys hunt pigs, deer, and monkeys, and fish for food. Traditionally, agriculture is considered women's work. Women grow bananas, yucca, sugarcane, and coca.

The Campa have much more contact with the outside world than the Jívaro, and this has influenced their culture. Occasionally a tribe can minimize the damage done to their culture by outside influences. For example, the Shipibo of central Peru, who live along the Ucayali River, have preserved their cultural identity although historically they have had many links with outsiders. They even have a cooperative selling their pottery and weavings to museums and shops from around the world.

Like the rest of Peru, the Amazonians also had problems with terrorists. In 1990 the Maoist terrorist group Sendero Luminoso killed the Ashaninka chief. In retaliation the Ashaninka declared war on the guerillas and drove all of them from their land.

CONFLICT WITH THE SPANISH

The history of the Jívaros is fairly representative of the Amazonian tribes. The Spanish tried to establish towns in the gold-abundant jungle areas, but taxed the Jívaro so heavily that it led to a massive rebellion in 1599. The Jívaro killed 20,000 to 30,000 Spanish, burned and sacked their towns, captured the Spanish governor, and tortured him in retaliation for his increasing tax demands. They poured molten gold down his throat until his bowels burst, saying they wanted to see whether he could get his fill of gold. But even though they could deter the Spanish, they could not withstand the diseases the Spanish brought. The natives retreated farther and farther into the interior, and the Spanish left them alone except for the unsuccessful attempts of missionaries.

For several hundred years there was peace, and then in the 19th century the boom in rubber brought Spanish rubber barons and their guns. Whole villages were destroyed by the rubber barons, who enslaved the remaining population. If any tribe or village was known to be particularly hostile, the barons surrounded the village and slaughtered its inhabitants. After 1912, however, the rubber market collapsed worldwide, and the natives were left alone again.

In the 1960s, however, the government settled highland peasants into the Amazon and opened the area to the exploitation of its hardwoods and petroleum. In the early 20th century nearly 40 tribes had never been contacted by outsiders; today there are probably only two or three.

MIGRATION WITHIN PERU

The poorer one is in Peru, the more likely one is to migrate. Those who migrate, either temporarily or permanently, do so from the Sierra to the coast and from the rural to the urban areas. At the beginning of the 20th century, Sierra natives were recruited for the coastal plantations and mines. Generally this has changed; the towns and cities have now become the main locus of migration. More rarely, Serranos may go to the Selva for the harvest season because the tropical harvesttime is during the Sierra off-season.

Mestizos are different from the indigenous people in that they tend to migrate from towns in the Sierra to towns on the coast. Theirs is usually a permanent or long-term migration. With the elite migration to the United States is more common, while migration within Peru is less common because most of the people of this class already reside on the coast. However, due to government land redistribution, the elite's dominance in the Sierra has eroded. As a result, some members of the elite have retired to the coast where their children have taken jobs in the service sector, such as media or finance.

Earlier in the 20th century, coastal mines or plantations were the main choices for migrants, but from the 1960s onward, Lima has been the main target destination. It is a cumulative process—Serranos move to Lima because relatives or friends are there. Over the years, associations and clubs have sprung up to organize migrants, helping them secure jobs and obtain housing. The housing has usually been in squatter camps called *pueblos jóvenes* (PWEB-lohs HOE-ven-es), or "young towns." As a community, the settlers arrange their own services until the local government helps them. Despite poor wages and very basic housing, many migrants still find better services and wages on the coast than in the Sierra.

Migration has helped to change the lot of the poorest classes in Peru by putting them in touch with a much larger section of society than they would previously have had contact with within the Sierra. Natives who come to the coast frequently learn Spanish, become literate, join unions, vote, and gain experience in a cash economy, rather than the barter system they knew. When these migrants return to the Sierra, they take with them the skills to deal with the outside world and to negotiate with local employers and plantation owners. They also become their communities' intermediaries through whom other native Serranos can articulate their wishes.

In the 1960s and 1970s, Lima was the destination of large numbers of migrants from rural areas. As the urban authorities could not provide adequate cheap housing, the migrants built simple shelters out of reed mats. The squatters demanded basic amenities like water and electricity and soon learned that protest marches were more effective than petitions.

Traditional weaving techniques are in danger of disappearing. Because the middle and upper classes and those who aspire to these classes have a general dislike of natives, traditional native dress is looked down upon. The brightly colored and multipatterned varieties of poncho and manta, or shoulder wrap, are giving way to black and brown varieties, which are considered socially superior.

CLOTHES MAKE THE PERSON

People who live in the cities and towns, as well as mestizos who live in rural areas, wear Western dress. Traditional dress is more frequently worn by natives in the rural areas.

The Spanish changed every aspect of native life when they came to Peru. That included introducing new materials such as sheep's wool (the Incas used alpaca wool) and silk. Tailoring was also introduced. During the 1570s and 1580s and after the native revolts of the late 18th century, the Spanish issued edicts forbidding the wearing of traditional clothing, which was a sign of native nationalism to the Spanish. By around 1700 a native man with high social status would wear European-style clothing, whereas the women persisted in wearing Inca-style dress.

NATIVE MEN'S DRESS   Contemporary native dress is a mixture of Western and Incan. Men's pants and shirt are European. The shirt, called *kutun* (KOO-tun), is made of wool or cotton and usually factory-made or made by local market tailors. The pants, or *pantalones* (pan-tah-LO-nes), are made from handwoven flannel-like wool cloth of one color, usually black, which is called *bayeta* (bay-YET-ah). A *bayeta* vest or waistcoat is sometimes worn over a shirt, called a *chaleco* (cha-LEH-koh). Sandals are made either of tire rubber or leather and, if not made in the home, can be found in most markets.

Each village has different patterns or colors associated with it that are reproduced on the costumes, and this applies to hats as well. Brimmed hats called *monteras* (mon-TEH-rahs) are very common and are worn by natives and *cholos*. The style is reminiscent of Spanish colonial hats. A more traditional version is the *chullo* (CHOO-yoh), a handknit hat with ear flaps that is sometimes worn under the *montera*. It is usually brightly colored and can be decorated with buttons. Originally the *chullo* came from the Aymará people, but it can now be seen all over the highlands.

PONCHOS

Originating from the Incas, the poncho worn in the Peruvian Andes is longer than the version worn in Chile. Ponchos are made of two pieces of cloth woven from alpaca or sheep's wool, sewn together with a hole left in the middle for the head. Every locality has an individual style, with distinctive colors, motifs, and patterns. Elaborate patterns have been developed over the last 400 years. Incan designs feature geometric patterns and use motifs of llamas, birds, and men. The
Spanish introduced horses, butterflies, and the double-headed bird—the Hapsburg eagle. It has been estimated that the time it takes to spin, dye, and weave a traditional poncho is around 500 to 600 hours over a period of as long as six months. Because of this great effort, one poncho is generally given to a person on entering adulthood and is expected to last a lifetime.

Aymará dancers during wedding festivities. One of the most interesting sights in the highlands is the brightly colored bowler hat worn by some natives. Adapted from the British bowler hat around 1900, they have become a favorite with natives. The colors denote the wearer's locality.

NATIVE WOMEN'S DRESS Women wear their hair in two braids, which are then tied together at the back. Like the men, they wear a *montera* and sandals. The skirt, or *pollera* (po-YEH-rah), is a full-gathered wool skirt, usually with a decorated hem. Traditionally they are black, but they can be found in navy blue, pink, yellow, or orange. On festival days, a woman will wear as many *pollera* as possible to signify her wealth. Most women own only one or two. Around Cuzco, a short jacket, or *saco* (SAH-koh), which is ornamented with braids and buttons, is worn. The belt is the same as a man's.

A manta, worn by nearly every woman as a shawl, is a rectangular or square piece of handwoven cloth. If a village has a particular color or design on its ponchos, it is usually repeated on the manta. To keep the manta in place, a *tupo* (TOO-poh), or small pin, is used. This has a flat, hammered, circular head with knife-sharp edges. The pins vary in design and can be in the shape of flowers or birds and trees. Depending on what class the woman belongs to, the pin will be made of copper, silver, or gold. Also commonly used is the safety pin.

LIFESTYLE

PRESENT-DAY PERUVIANS LIVE IN a rapidly changing society. Recent economic upheavals, combined with intense urban migration and improvements in transportation and communications, have had a profound effect on the lives of many Peruvians.

Old ways are disappearing or being adapted to new influences. Changes in women's roles, the growth of the middle class, and public education are bringing new opportunities to the entire population.

As a nation, Peruvians have long experience in adapting to changing influences. Under the domination of the Incas and later the Spanish, Peru's people have learned to resist oppression and renew themselves in adverse conditions. Like their ancestors, modern Peruvians are once again experiencing the process of resisting and renewing.

Left: **A couple waiting to be married in Cuzco.**

Opposite: **A local man dressed in a traditional Andes costume plays a pipe flute at the Chincero Sunday market.**

65

A girl helps her mother remove a donkey-load of onions in Cuzco.

ROLES OF WOMEN AND MEN

Peru is generally a man's world, and the Hispanic concept of machismo (ma-CHEES-moh), which defines masculine attributes and the firm belief in male superiority, is paramount in the Peruvian culture. Machismo is a point of distinction for a South American male. It creates the image of someone who is strong and respected, in addition to being protective and providing well for his wife and family. There is a persistent double standard in the treatment of men and women. Whereas men may have a mistress or lover, women are strictly forbidden to do this. Whereas a man can divorce his wife because of her adultery, a woman generally cannot do the same unless there is a public scandal.

As it is a Hispanic concept, machismo is not practiced by the native peoples. The Quechua still practice trial marriage, where women and men choose their partners and can end the relationship when they so wish. The woman is free to enter another marriage with no stigma attached to her. Any children resulting from the union are regarded as belonging to the community as a whole.

The 1993 constitution guarantees the equality of women and provides laws that do not discriminate against them. The Domestic Workers Law, passed in 2003, outlines basic rights, such as requiring employers to provide health care.

Government enforcement of its own laws has been problematic, however, as statistics show that only 40 percent of domestic helpers are receiving the health care they are entitled to. In today's Peruvian society, women from all walks of life still face traditional barriers deriving from machismo that impede their social and business prospects.

According to statistics, the female share of the labor force has changed over the last few decades. In 1970 women formed 20 percent of the workforce, in 1995 they made up 30 percent, and by 2002 the figure was 49.7 percent.

In addition many of the jobs held by women, such as those in street stalls, informal employment, or domestic work, are not reflected in these statistics. Faced with the economic downfall of the late 1990s, many women have been forced to supplement the family income by working part-time or setting up street stalls. Middle-class women have started their own businesses or entered professional careers.

The feminist movement is relatively new to Peru. It is essentially a movement pertaining to well-educated, middle-class urban women, since most other organizations have a left-wing bias that deters elite women from joining. Most of these groups are restricted to helping urban women by providing legal and educational ways to improve the treatment of women.

A recent survey by the World Health Organization (WHO) showed that 31 percent of women of middle- and low-income backgrounds in Lima had reported at least one case of physical assault in the previous year. The true figure is likely higher, as many such crimes go unreported due to the fear of further retaliation. Police suspect that only 10 percent of crimes committed against women are reported.

Flora Tristan, the daughter of a Peruvian noble, was a renowned feminist and socialist who advocated free love, divorce, and the abolition of slavery in her Peregrinations of a Pariah.

A Quechua wedding. By the time a couple marries, they may have several children, who cannot be baptized until their parents are married.

FAMILY

The family is the most important social unit in Peru and forms the center of the community. Singlehood is unusual and deemed unacceptable. There is little socialization between people who are not kin.

There are regional and socioeconomic differences as to what constitutes a household. However, a group composed of several siblings and their respective spouses is usually the basic domestic unit. Most often children live with their families until they marry and, sometimes, even afterward as well. Young men and women from upper-middle and upper-class families sometimes get their own apartments before they are married, but it is more common for newlyweds to live with one of their large families until enough is saved to set up house for themselves. Individuals in these families may own separate belongings, but generally the house and land are of common ownership and land is farmed and tended together if it is located in a rural environment.

The family cycle begins with the marriage. The arrangement can be very flexible for some in the lower classes and the Quechua. Often an alliance between a couple is arranged by their parents, but it is initiated because of the couple's choice. Next they enter a period of *sirvinakuy* (seer-veen-ah-KEE), meaning "to serve each other," during which the woman works with her mother-in-law and the man with his father-in-law. This is a test of their readiness for marriage. During this stage they may sleep together under

the same roof, usually with the man's family. The couple generally does not marry until a child is conceived, showing the union to be fruitful, and even then might postpone the wedding for a long time. Weddings are frequently ornate and expensive occasions that take years to finance.

A patriarchal system exists within the family, where the father is the head of the household. Young men achieve independence from their fathers only gradually over a period of years. Even among brothers, the eldest takes precedence. Boys generally inherit from their fathers and girls from their mothers. As the parents grow older, they usually loosen their authoritative hold on the family.

Migration to urban areas can weaken the ties of rural families, making them less complete and less extended. The migrants are also cut off from a family base. To compensate for this isolation, they move to places where relatives have previously migrated.

Because race is so important in determining one's social class and socioeconomic position, family background or a good family name is one of the key aspects of life. Families descended from the 16th century Spanish settlers are more than proud of this fact. If the family has a crest or coat of arms, this is proudly displayed above the door of their home.

In Peru family means more than just the immediate family. It includes a wide, extended kinship circle of several generations. A typical couple is likely to have between three and six children.

PATRONAGE

Hispanic countries have a tradition of strong, tight-knit families, and Peru is no exception. In the world of business, this is often extended so that family members are incorporated into firms that may be family-run or publicly owned. Although nepotism is not considered appropriate in North America, such patronage in Peru is seen to be perfectly reasonable.

One of the principal reasons for patronage is that an employer who selects family members for the job knows the strengths and weaknesses of the individuals being hired, often having known them all their lives and perhaps their parents as well. The employer can thus match them to jobs that suit their skills accurately. The employer can also trust family members more than strangers, and the employees in return work to the best of their abilities out of family loyalty. It is considered unthinkable for an employer to look outside his or her family or for somebody not intimately known when hiring.

In some ways the system of patronage is detrimental to business because it can prevent new talents and ideas from entering a firm. It can dissuade more talented people who are not family members from making a positive contribution to the family. Few positions of importance will ever be given to those who are not family members.

GODPARENTS

Social life revolves around the family, and its importance is paramount. To offset this influence and connect the family with the outside world, godparents are chosen for children for the major religious and social events in their lives. Baptism, the first haircut, and marriage are the main events for which they are chosen.

A child might have several sets of godparents during his or her lifetime, but those chosen for baptism are the most important. Having godparents was originally a Hispanic custom, but it is also practiced by the native peoples today.

Depending on the region in which they live, the duties of godparents vary, but generally when their godchildren are baptized, gifts are given to the parents and children and a contribution is made to a fiesta if the family decides to hold one.

Godparents are meant to give a good start in life to their godchildren, especially in the godchildren's formative years. As a godchild grows up, godparents are less obliged to help in the upbringing of the child unless the child is in serious trouble. It is meant to be a lifelong relationship of great love and respect.

Sometimes when a godchild is orphaned, he or she is raised by a godparent. Social and emotional ties are created, and the serious obligations of the godparent are paid back by the child's love and respect.

People within or outside the family can be chosen as godparents, but generally it is better for a well-off person, a hacienda (ranch) owner, boss, or prominent mestizo to be chosen. In the native community this is a way of linking the family to the wider community and society at large.

For the poor it acknowledges their dependence on the rich, and this in turn obliges the rich to better the lot of the less fortunate.

Godchildren call their godfather *padrino* (pah-DREE-no) and their godmother *madrina* (mah-DREE-nah), and the parents of the children call the godparents *compadre* (com-PAH-dray) and *comadre* (com-MAH-dray), respectively. These affectionate names indicate the closeness of the relationship both for the children and for their parents.

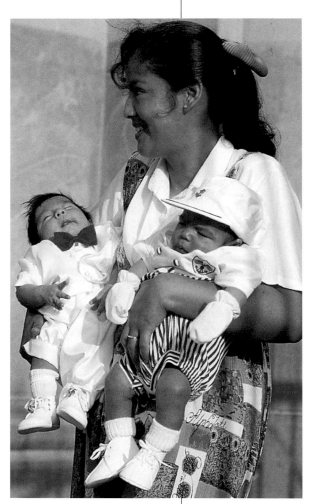

A woman holds two babies before the start of their baptismal ceremony.

71

ROLES WITHIN THE FAMILY

The father is the head and authority in the household. He expects his wife to be obedient and attentive to his wishes. In return, he shields his wife and children from harm or social disgrace. He must maintain the good name of the family.

In a country where the machismo culture is strong, the Peruvian woman has to perform many roles: a good wife, a mother, and a hostess. She manages the household, not just cooking and cleaning, but also entertaining visitors or her husband's clients or employers. In upper-class families, a wife who performs these difficult duties with style and grace is considered a real asset to her husband's career. However, society considers a wife's main duty to be that of looking after the children, educating them morally and socially. (In the picture, a woman teaches her daughter to weave.) Although upper-class, educated women can find professional employment, gender inequality continues to be a problem. In the lower classes, financial strains force more and more women to seek employment, often as domestic helpers or street stall vendors. These jobs are usually undocumented and low-paying.

The rise of the terrorist group Sendero Luminoso in the 1980s abruptly changed the traditional role of women in Peru. Attacks in the Andes and the Amazon disrupted everyday living and caused many to migrate from these areas. This left the women in charge of organizing migrant families, and as many as 78 percent of households were headed by a woman. In many of Lima's shanty towns, it was the women who organized breakfast clubs and mothers' clubs to feed their families. At a time when rebel and military threats were crippling the power of trade unions and political parties, these women-run organizations provided many female community leaders.

In urban Peru the gender divide is slowly changing. The number of female students in universities is almost the same as their male counterparts. Their presence is increasingly felt in the banking, legal, and academic professions. In the rural communities, however, the attitude toward women remains extremely traditional.

HEALTH

Peruvians' health is generally improving, but health care is disproportionately weighted toward the coast and Lima, where transportation and communication infrastructures are stronger and better established. Latest figures from 2002 show that the government health program receives just 2.4 percent of the national budget, a figure that has been in steady decline.

Like other Latin American nations, Peru's public health system faces problems, but is getting better. The 2002 Joint Monitoring Program for Water Supply and Sanitation by WHO and UNICEF estimated that 84 percent of the urban population had access to safe drinking water in their households, while 40 percent of those living in rural areas had the same access. The country's infant mortality rate has decreased over the past 35 years, from 108 per thousand births in 1970, to 52 in 1992, and 32 in 2005.

Risk of death from malnutrition, septicemia (blood poisoning), and acute diarrhea was 8 to 10 times greater for children living in extreme poverty. In 2000 the rate of anemia among children under 5 years of age and women 15 to 49 years of age was 50 percent and 30 percent, respectively. Poor sanitation is a continual threat to public health, although the prevalence of sanitation facilities is rising. Figures from 2000 show 79 percent of the urban population has adequate sanitation facilities, in contrast to 49 percent of the rural population. Average life expectancy has increased over the last few decades and, as of 2005, stands at 69.53 years (67.77 male, 71.37 female).

Malnutrition is one of the main causes of the high infant mortality rate. Eleven percent of all newborns are underweight because of the mother's malnutrition.

73

Schoolchildren in an isolated Andean village near Cuzco department.

EDUCATION

A good economy grows out of a well-educated workforce. Although primary and secondary education enrollment levels have increased greatly, those of university or technical education beyond high school have stalled. Additionally, families living in poverty often have little choice but to remove their older children from school so they can work and help feed the family. As a result, although almost all children enroll in primary school, those from lower socioeconomic backgrounds are far less likely to graduate. As many as 20 percent of students in the final grade of primary school are not enrolled in high school. In rural areas fewer girls enroll in secondary schools because of gender bias.

One of the vital indicators of education quality is the ratio of teachers to students. This has consistently improved from the 1970 figure of 35 pupils per teacher in primary schools, to 28 in 1990, and 25 in 2003. The percentage of students enrolled in school has also increased. For primary education, 88 percent of children of school-going age were enrolled in 1990 and this rose to 100 percent in 2003. What is noteworthy is that enrollment figures give little indication of actual attendance. Numbers in secondary education remained relatively stable at 70 percent in 1990 and 69 percent in 2003. For college education, the figure dipped from 36 percent in 1990 to 32 percent in 2003. Adult literacy is up from 85.1 percent in 1990 (91.5 percent men, 78.7 percent women) to 87.7 percent in 2004 (93.5 percent men, 82.1 percent women). GDP expenditure for education dropped substantially from 3.09 percent in 1980 to 2.29 percent in 1990,

but recent figures reveal education spending had increased to 3 percent in 2003, making up about 17.1 percent of total government expenditure. Preschool education or day care is provided for children below the age of 6. The 2003 enrollment rate was 58 percent.

Going to school in Lima. In spite of its attempts to educate Peruvians, the government is falling behind because of the growth of the school-age population.

The Peruvian system breaks down basic education into three cycles, with students proceeding to the next cycle on completion of the previous one. Education is obligatory from ages 6 to 16, during which time students are expected to complete their basic education.

In rural areas lessons in the early years are conducted in the native language, usually Quechua or Aymará. Spanish is taught in the upper grades. Many children live in remote areas far from schools, so a system of *núcleos* (NOO-klay-ohs) was developed. Scattered throughout the country, *núcleos* serve the needs of several nearby communities and can teach all three cycles of the basic education program. Although the *núcleos* have increased enrollment levels, critics are quick to note that low wages paid by the government have yielded unskilled teachers.

A VILLAGE IN THE ANDES

The road to a typical village in the Andes is usually narrow and made of earth, baked hard in the summer and turned muddy from torrents of rain in the winter. A network of narrow roads runs over the mountains, connecting small, isolated villages, but in bad weather these roads can be totally impassable. Old buses and heavy trucks use these roads in addition to pack animals such as llamas.

At the end of such a road, the village is mainly inhabited by Quechua who have lived in the same way for a thousand years in much the same manner as Europeans who lived in the Middle Ages. The few concessions to modern living are Western dress, running water (still rare), metal pots and pans, radios, and flashlights. Crops and livestock introduced by the Spanish have also been adopted.

Electricity is rare, as only big villages have a generator. A village is more likely to have safe drinking water from a few taps dotted throughout the village. If not, people have to trek to the nearest stream or spring several times a day to carry water back.

A field in the Urubamba Valley. Village life is hard and simple, with most villagers surviving on subsistence agriculture.

The crops a village grows depends on the altitude of the village. A village high in the mountains grows potatoes and a few grains and keeps herds of llamas, sheep, goats, and, if they are relatively wealthy, some cattle. On the lower levels, lemons, limes, avocados, and chilies are cultivated in addition to ordinary vegetables. The crops are usually planted from low to high altitude, and harvested in the reverse order.

Houses are typically made of earthen bricks baked in the sun or, in rare cases, stone. The dwellings usually have one or two rooms that are roofed with a heavy thatch of puna grasses. The floors are made of hardened earth, and cooking is done in a hearth in the center of the floor. The houses are often smoky from the hearth fire, and the undersides of roofs are black and sooty. There is little furniture beyond a stool or two. A comparatively wealthy family might have a locally made, rough-hewn bed or table. The bed is usually a pallet covered with blankets and sheepskins. In a prosperous home there might be a bed frame with a mattress of bundled reeds.

Women squat on the floor; men sit on benches made from earth. Families own very few personal items: clothing, pots and pans, tools and farming implements, their house, a little land, and, most important, the battery-run radio.

People in the Andes begin their day to the sound of the radio. There are over 550 radios stations in Peru but the one the highlanders listen to is Radio Tawantinsuyu, where DJs speak in Quechua and folk music starts the day. Much of its broadcasting is dedicated to reading personal messages to distant villagers who have no telephone. For people who live in a remote village and only occasionally visit small market towns, a radio is almost a magical connection with the rest of a very strange, foreign world.

Towns or large villages in the highlands are often the result of a policy pursued by the Spanish viceroy Francisco de Toledo in the 1570s. The Spanish gathered together all the natives living in scattered communities and moved them into one town in order to control and tax them more efficiently. It was also easier to force the natives to convert to Catholicism. The settlements were called *reducciones* (ray-duc-SYO-nays), which means reductions.

Reducciones were laid out according to a special plan. A good site was picked for the town at the right altitude, near a stream or spring, with enough room to build a church, a cobbled main street, and at least one official building. Each family's house had a street-facing door so that the family could be monitored.

Compared to the time of their initial settlement, the populations of many *reducciones* are much smaller today. After some years, the natives often slipped away and went back to

A native woman prepares food in an Inca-style house in the Andes.

their old homes and communities. Such migration began after the towns were created and has continued for 400 years.

A DAY IN THE ANDES

The woman of the house is the first to rise, stirring last night's embers into a fire and then putting on the kettle to brew some *mate* (mah-tay), a sort of herbal tea. At breakfast, which is around dawn, *mate* is served to the family with either *mote* (MOH-tay), boiled dried corn, or, more rarely, bread.

As the family eats breakfast the mother prepares lunch, or *almuerzo* (al-MWER-zo), which is eaten when most people in North America would be eating their breakfast. *Almuerzo* consists of a thick soup of potatoes and other vegetables, a hot sauce made of chilies, and a mug of *chicha* (CHEE-chah), a beer made of fermented corn. This meal is served to all the workers in the household, who would usually gather in the kitchen. These might include fathers, sons, and grandfathers. There may also be godparents of their children or just neighbors who owe the family a day's work in return for the family's earlier labor in their fields. After eating, the men go to the fields and work steadily throughout the day. In order to complete the tasks before nightfall, they will only take occasional breaks.

When the men have left, the mother begins to prepare the third meal of the day, which is more complex and plentiful than the other two. It includes two or three dishes with the usual potatoes and *mote*, but with the addition of meat as a special thanks to the men helping her family.

If the job the men are carrying out in the field is a communal one, the woman may be assisted in her task by the wives or mothers of the field hands. She is also expected to look after the children, milk the cow, lead it to pasture, and feed the chickens and pigs.

Around noon she packs the meal with all the utensils, plates, spoons, and maybe a bottle or two of *trago* (TRAH-goh), a cane liquor, and *chicha,* and leaves for the fields with the children and other women. After the men have eaten and drunk their fill, they return to work.

The women will either sit and watch while drinking *chicha* and playing with the children, or they will work in the fields themselves, plowing, hoeing, or reaping. The children drink an unfermented and sweetened *chicha* that comes in two flavors–*chichi blanca*, made from white corn, and *chicha morada*, made from purple corn.

At the end of the day, which is usually twilight, everything is gathered up and they all go home. Cattle, sheep, or goats are herded up and taken back also. At home they drink a last cup of *chicha* before the beds are laid out. The fire is reduced to a few glowing embers that will light the next day's kindling, and the family goes to bed.

RELIGION

ALTHOUGH PERU DOES NOT have an official religion, most people in the country consider themselves Roman Catholic. For the native peoples, however, Catholicism incorporates much of the former Incan religious beliefs.

The majestic mountains that surround them are considered to have spirits, offerings are still made to the earth, and images of the sun still figure prominently in religious iconography. For the people of the Andes, Incan beliefs and Catholic doctrine have fused into a harmonious whole in which the festival of Saint John the Baptist conveniently coincides with the old Incan festival for the winter solstice, and traditional marriage customs naturally accommodate a church wedding.

ANCIENT PERUVIAN BELIEFS

The religion of the ancient Incas permeated all aspects of public and private life. They worshipped many gods, goddesses, and spirits, each of which was responsible for a different aspect of life.

Viracocha was the most important god, having created the sun, moon, stars, earth, oceans, and weather—in fact, all natural things. Like many Incan gods, Viracocha is neither male nor female, nor just one being. The god's complexity is apparent when one considers his or her responsibility both for water and fire.

Illapa was another important god representing thunderbolts, lightning, rain, hail, snow, and frost. He was venerated mainly in the highlands. Together with his son and his brother, they were depicted as the deities of the mountains.

Above: **Shamanistic ceremonial ground in the coastal desert, used since prehistoric times.**

Opposite: **Believers dressed in purple at "the Lord of the Miracles" procession in Lima.**

The sun god had the most elaborate temple in ancient Cuzco. Its walls were covered in gold and silver plate, and solid gold statues adorned its halls. Sacrifices and rites often took place here, as well as at the temples of Viracocha and Illapa. Rituals were intended to placate the gods and ward off cataclysms. Sacrifices were made of birds, llamas, guinea pigs, coca, corn, and sometimes even people, although this was rare and reserved for times of great suffering.

The Incas inherited aspects of earlier religions as well as beliefs from newly conquered regions, but they superimposed their own brand of mysticism on them. This helped conquered peoples adapt because they were able to keep their own gods while admitting the superiority of Viracocha and the sun.

The god Pachacamac ruled over the lowlands and the underworld, causing earthquakes and pestilence. He was represented as a golden fox. Another god was Amaru, a serpent who rose from the underworld. Amaru symbolized the communication between the living and the dead.

Some deities were exclusively female. These included Killa, the moon, who was the wife of the sun. Statues of her were made of silver, and those of the sun were of gold. Killa was associated with the earth and death.

The center of the Incan religion was undoubtedly the sun god, Inti. Although not as powerful as Viracocha, the sun was more physical and less mystical.

The emperors at Cuzco demanded to be recognized as direct descendants of the sun. It was believed that this exalted lineage would give them a semidivine status, as well as an excuse for military subjugation of other regions. After all, the sun reigned over the highlands (considered the center of the empire) and the heavens. He was viewed as a paternalistic god who planned for the welfare of the universe and its people, the Incas, while controlling their every action.

THE NAZCA LINES

The Nazca Lines, giant drawings in a desert in the south of Peru, were created by the Nazca people, likely sometime between B.C. 200 and A.D. 600. The lines cover such a wide area that they are only properly visible from the air. Several dozen figures, mostly animals, are represented: a 600-foot (183-m) lizard, a 300-foot (90-m) monkey with a tightly curled tail, and a condor with a 400-foot (122-m) wingspan. (The picture below shows the hummingbird.) The lines were created by removing the top layer of earth to reveal the lighter-colored dust beneath. Other designs include triangles, rectangles, and straight lines that run across the desert. The longest line is more than 5.5 miles (over 9 km) long. The area was declared a UNESCO World Cultural Heritage site in 1994.

Maria Reiche (*above*), devoted her life to studying the lines. She theorized that they represented a giant calendar corresponding to solar and lunar movements, and the constellations.

While Reiche's theory is the most well known, there are several others, none of which is widely accepted. The purpose behind the Nazca Lines remains a mystery.

Before she passed away at the age of 95, Maria Reiche (1903–98) was a fierce protector of the lines, many times single-handedly shielding them from vandals and from government plans to build irrigation ditches, to reconstruct the lines, and to develop roadways and other forms of unsustainable tourism.

The Cathedral of Lima sits on the site chosen by Pizarro, but has been reconstructed several times after earthquakes.

THE ROMAN CATHOLIC CHURCH

Peru is a highly Catholic country, with 81 percent of the population professing to be Roman Catholic. Seventh Day Adventists account for 1.4 percent, other Christians 0.7 percent, and other religions 0.6 percent. Around 16.3 percent do not claim a faith or are atheist or agnostic. Often Catholicism is combined with native myths and legends. Catholic festivals were usually substituted for the Incan religious festivals on the same date, so the two inevitably became mixed. The Incan religion and other native religions linger on in the mountains and jungles.

Peru's history and destiny have been profoundly shaped by the Roman Catholic Church. The church reached Peru with Francisco Pizarro in 1533, and a few years later, in 1537, the diocese of Cuzco was established. The church quickly founded hospitals, including a 12-room hospital in Lima for natives, and built schools. Almost 60 schools were established by 1548, and in 1551 the University of San Marcos in Lima was created.

Schools were part of the church's campaign to convert the natives. This method started immediately with the Spanish arrival. Many obstacles, including the varied forms of local cults and the inaccessibility of the native population, made this conversion difficult.

Although they were the prime target of conversion, native peoples were excluded from becoming priests until the 17th century. Mestizos and Creoles (a person of European descent who was born in Spanish America) made up the majority of the clergy. Foreign priests from Spain and elsewhere in Latin America have often been needed because of a dramatic decline in the number of priests since the 19th century. Until as recently as 1963, 70 percent of bishops were foreign. In 1821 there was one priest for every 500 people. Today there is one priest for every 10,000 people.

The 17th century was known as the religious century. The church was at the pinnacle of the artistic and intellectual culture it had helped to create. Many sculptures, paintings, and the grand colonial cathedrals were all made at the behest of the church. Two saints were also canonized during this period, the most famous being Saint Rose (Santa Rosa) of Lima (1586–1617). The first saint to be canonized in the Americas, her sympathy for the native peoples made her Peru's originator of social services. Another Peruvian saint, Saint Martin (San Martín) de Porres (1579–1639) was the first black saint. A district in Lima is named after him.

The altar of San Pedro Church in Lima.

Peruvian soldiers carry a saint's litter in a procession around the streets.

CHURCH AND STATE

The church in Peru has always been involved in social matters, which has occasionally conflicted with the state's interest. Formerly, priests often told people how they ought to vote. During the campaign for independence in the 1800s, the clergy (mainly consisting of mestizos) supported the revolutionaries against the Spanish.

In 1845 Catholicism was made the official state religion. Foreigners were permitted to conduct their own services, but no Peruvians were allowed to attend. The 1920 constitution gave individuals freedom of religion, which was subsequently reaffirmed in the 1979 constitution. In the constitution of 1933 and in amendments made in 1940 and 1961, the state declared that the country was no longer officially or formally Roman Catholic. Despite this, the church was given special status, and religious instruction is still obligatory in all educational institutions in the country.

Although it has been one of the more conservative churches in Latin America, the Peruvian church has increasingly supported socially progressive movements and has proposed reforms. The military coup of 1968 was supported by the church because of the military's agrarian policy, which nationalized most property. The coup unleashed a reborn dedication to social reform, which is presently doing much to alleviate the condition of the peasants. This has meant criticizing the present government. A consequence has been an increase in the church's popularity with the poor. When the late Pope John Paul II visited in 1985 and 1988, vast public rallies were held in celebration.

The church is such a large and varied institution in Peru that at times it can appear to be both critical and supportive of the government because of differing views among different factions within the church.

Opposition to the church has come from both the right and the left, the government and military as well as Sendero Luminoso. The church's social projects have been destroyed, and there have been cases of priests being killed by both sides.

TWO REMARKABLE SAINTS

Peru is the birthplace of two saints of particular importance to the Americas: Saint Rose of Lima and Saint Martin de Porres.

Saint Martin de Porres was born in Lima in 1579, the illegitimate son of a noble Spaniard and a black woman. It was not customary at that time to allow a mulatto to enter a religious order in Peru, but because of his exceptional qualities and virtue he was admitted to the Dominican Order in 1610. Martin was known for his kindness to all people, especially to the poor and the unfortunate. He was also a special friend to animals. He established an orphanage and a school for the youth of Lima, which is considered his monument. His feast day is November 5.

Saint Rose of Lima was the first person born in the New World to be canonized by the Catholic Church and is called the patron saint of the Americas and the Philippines. She was born in Lima in 1586. Although her mother wanted her to marry, Rose was determined to devote her life to religion, and in 1606 her mother relented and Rose became a nun, living in seclusion in a hut on the family property. Her feast day is August 30.

The Peruvian Catholic Church has made special efforts to reach the people in the last few decades. Masses are conducted in Quechua, Aymará, and other dialects. In Villa El Salvador, a shantytown south of Lima, Father Eugene Kirk, an Irish priest, said, "Many don't understand Quechua, but they are so dumbfounded a foreigner speaks it that they reconsider their parents' language. There is a perpetual process of reevaluation."

Catholicism is still influential with the lower classes, and the parish church is still considered the center of the community.

MODERN RELIGIOUS PRACTICE

Although Peru is overwhelmingly Catholic, people display only nominal allegiance to the church. Only 15 percent of Peruvian Roman Catholics attend mass weekly. Most people practice "popular Catholicism," which means occasionally attending special events like the sacraments, festivals, processions, or saints' days. Among the middle and upper classes, religion is losing its importance. Some are alienated by the church's renewed extremism, such as opposition to birth control.

Fiestas celebrating saints' days or religious holidays are an important aspect of community life and break the routine of hard work. Each landworking family in the peasant community takes turns paying for a given fiesta of that year, usually at great personal expense.

The church has done much to integrate Spanish and Incan beliefs. Although Spanish Catholic festivals replaced Incan ones, remnants of Incan beliefs still exist. In the Sierra old traditions abound, and healers would talk with spirits to diagnose diseases and prescribe herbal medicines.

SHAMANISM: MAGIC AND CURE

Shamanism has been popular for over 3,000 years. As a developing country, most of Peru's population cannot afford or even have access to doctors or proper medical care. Many people, especially the natives and the poor, rely on the shaman's ancient healing art or *curandero* (kur-ahn-DAIR-oh), the rural spiritual healer. Even former President Fernando Belaúnde's family employed one. The shaman can be found in every large community, principally in the Sierra and the Selva. People may travel hundreds of miles to see one. The people of the Amazon region have best maintained the shamanistic culture and spiritual traditions.

Shamanism uses herbs and hands-on therapy to cure people not just from physical sickness but from fear, jealousy, tension, and anger. The treatment draws on the combined spiritual and magical elements of native culture. It attempts to treat one's overall wellness rather than just the symptoms of illnesses.

Most shamans use hallucinogens (potent drugs extracted from plants) that the Incas previously used. Under the hallucinogen's influence, a patient experiences revelation, a period when the shaman asks the person questions and sets tasks that are interpreted to reveal the source of the illness. Shamans also consume the drug themselves in order to see into the future, recover lost souls, and find lost objects. Sometimes the whole community participates. Traditional spirit-songs are sung to enable them to get in touch with the ancestors' spirit world. In a way the shaman acts as a conserving force against the discordances of modern life and the encroaching industrial world, preserving a tribe's culture as established by their ancestors. (Below is a picture of a shaman ceremony at the Inti Raymi Festival.)

SE REPARAN
TODA MARCA
DE RELOJES

LANGUAGE

WITH THE SPANISH CONQUEST in the 16th century, the Spanish language quickly rose to prominence in Peru. Native peoples were accustomed to having rulers who spoke a different language. Indeed, the Spanish conquest was helped by the fact that the Incan emperors and their court at Cuzco spoke a different language from their subjects, who thus felt little allegiance to them.

Today, Spanish is the official language of Peru. People of the highlands generally speak Quechua or Aymará, and the native peoples of the Amazon region speak languages from 12 different linguistic families. In addition to these language variations, there is also Creole slang. Linguistically varied and used at all levels of society, Creole slang is a result of the rich mixture of cultural influences Peru has incorporated.

NATIVE LANGUAGES

Aymará is a regional language with few speakers, most of whom live around the southernmost part of Peru adjacent to Lake Titicaca. In comparison, many natives still speak Quechua, the ancient language of the Incas. It is popularly known to the native peoples as Runasimi, meaning "Mouth of the People." During the days of the Incan empire, it was spoken in the region that is modern-day Peru, Bolivia, Ecuador, and parts of Argentina and Chile. It continued to spread even after the Spanish invasion, but its use declined and is now confined to Peru and parts of Ecuador and Bolivia.

There are around 10 million Quechua speakers, with many concentrated in the south. Many are from the Andean highlands. It is the largest indigenous language to survive in the Americas and has given some words to the English language: llama, cóndor, puma, and pampa, among others.

Quechua has many regional varieties, a result of the immensity of the old Incan empire, which encompassed many different peoples. The purest

The word Indio *(in-DEE-oh), "Indian," is regarded as insulting. The Spanish word* indígena, *meaning "indigenous" or "native," is normally used instead.*

Opposite: **A Peruvian vendor manning his stall in the Pisac market. The handpainted words indicate that he repairs all types of watches.**

91

and most prestigious form of Quechua is now spoken around Cuzco, the former capital of the Incas.

For a long time, Quechua was seen as a backward language or a language of subversion. It was outlawed by the Spanish in 1780 after a peasant revolt, and it was even discouraged by Simón Bolívar. Despite this, it survived. For a time in the 1970s it even became the official language of Peru. This was quickly watered down; official recognition remains only in areas where it is widely spoken.

The Incas did not have a written language or alphabet. Instead they had *quipu* (KEE-poo), an elaborate system of knotted string. This simple system was effective in communicating complex pieces of information (including detailed censuses) used in administering a large empire.

During the 16th century the Spanish clergy tried to learn Quechua, so that they could record the Incas' past history and also convert the natives by translating the Bible into a common language that would be understood. They wrote Quechua in the Roman alphabet, and it has been written this way ever since. The first book that was printed in Peru was a catechism in Quechua, which the priests used to teach the natives.

SOME BASIC WORDS IN SPANISH AND QUECHUA

ENGLISH	SPANISH	QUECHUA
one	*uno*	*hoq*
two	*dos*	*iskay*
three	*tres*	*kinsa*
four	*cuatro*	*tawa*
five	*cinco*	*pisqa*
six	*seis*	*soqta*
seven	*siete*	*qanchis*
eight	*ocho*	*pusaq*
nine	*nueve*	*isqon*
ten	*diez*	*chunka*
good morning	*buenos días*	*rimay kullaiki tutamanta*
good evening	*buenas noches*	*rimay kullaiki kaituta*
yes	*sí*	*ari*
no	*no*	*manan*
hello	*¡hola!*	*napaykullayki!*
please	*por favor*	*ama jina kaychu*
thank you	*muchas gracias*	*anchata sulpaiky*
how are you?	*¿cómo esta usted?*	*allinllachu*
fine	*bien*	*allinllan*

Nearly all the countries in Latin America use Spanish as their official or main language, with the exception of Brazil, where Portuguese is spoken. After including the population of Spain and Spanish speakers in North America, there are more than 300 million people worldwide who speak Spanish. Spanish is one of the easiest romance languages to learn. It is spoken as it is written, and many words are similar to those of English. The word order is also similar. In addition, visitors are grateful that the Spanish in Latin America is spoken much more slowly than the Spanish in Spain.

A young couple talking in the park.

Peruvians are very open and friendly, and it is not surprising to see women walking arm in arm with other women, or men with men.

GREETINGS AND GESTURES

Men and women shake hands when meeting and parting. Men embrace close friends or pat them on the back. Women kiss one another on the cheek. When two women are introduced, they may kiss one another. The same is sometimes true of men and women. Elders and officials are greeted with their title and last name. Principal titles are *doctor, profesor, arquitecto* (ahr-kee-TEC-toh), or architect, and *ingeniero* (een-hain-YER-oh), which means engineer. Some Peruvians call foreigners *gringo* if a man or *gringa* if a woman. In Peru this is a normal form of address.

People discuss family and occupation when meeting someone. To rush in and talk about business is considered rude. Some topics of conversation can be difficult. Because of the recent political situation in Peru, politics can be a very touchy area. Another sensitive topic relates to a person's ancestry. Most Peruvians feel more comfortable being associated with their Spanish colonial background than their native heritage.

When Peruvians converse, they stand much closer to one another than people in the United States do. To back away is taken as an insult.

THE PRESS

The 1993 constitution guarantees media freedom. This upholds the right to information, opinion, expression, and dissemination of thought in any form and through any medium without prior authorization or censorship. However, Peru has suffered from a long history of political interferences. In 1974 the Peruvian press was nationalized, which immediately stopped critical reporting about the government. The papers were returned to private ownership in 1980, but the previous six years of government control had drastically damaged their quality. Escalating political violence in the 1980s caused civilian governments to once again exert pressure on the press to subdue reports, and the latter even excluded references to terrorism.

In 1990 the Fujimori government closed *El Diario*, considering it a supporter of the terrorist Sendero Luminoso. Between 1983 and 1991 numerous journalists were killed, 17 by government security forces. Today's record is no better: the National Association of Journalists of Peru (ANP) registered 66 press freedom violations in 2005. Around 70 journalists were threatened or physically attacked (compared to 54 in 2004), and two were murdered, reportedly for criticizing local politicians.

Around 38 newspapers are published in Peru. Most big cities in the country have a daily newspaper. Because of high illiteracy rates and distribution problems in the scattered villages and towns, papers are mainly circulated in the Lima area and other main cities.

Lima has around 23 newspapers, including *El Peruano*, which is the official government newspaper. The right-wing *El Comercio* is the highest selling daily.

ARTS

PERU HAS MANY CULTURES. Thousands of years before the Europeans arrived, pre–Columbian New World civilizations such as the Andes Incas came and went in the area that is now Peru. Over the centuries many civilizations contributed to a diverse, dynamic, and thriving culture. Racial and geographic factors produced a regionalism in the arts: the Amazonian natives retain their cultural independence, the urbanized coast is greatly influenced by Europe, whereas the Sierra still preserves the flavor of the Incan empire. Probably the only area of artistic expression that all of Peru's people share is the art inspired by the Catholic Church.

NATIVE AND SPANISH: TWO SEPARATE ARTS

Peru's artistic achievements fall into four periods: pre-Incan, Incan, colonial, and postcolonial. There was little disruption between the pre-Incan and Incan periods, but colonization brought increasing tension and division in the artistic world between the traditional native cultures and the new. The Spanish conquerors destroyed much of the artwork created by the Incas. Nearly all the metalwork done in gold or silver was melted down. The Spanish imposed their own culture, destroying native art and traditions. For centuries after the conquest, the arts were little more than a direct imitation of Spanish styles. Ironically, the church often employed native artisans to carve statues and decorate interiors.

After independence from Spain, Creoles tried to forge a new artistic culture distinct from the Spanish as well as from the native culture. They began to look toward the whole of Europe rather than just to Spain. It was only in the early 20th century that Peruvians began to appreciate their artistic heritage. In present-day Peru, European influences and the indigenous past remain as two separate, often conflicting artistic strands.

Above: **A pre-Columbian textile from the Paracas necropolis culture, around A.D. 400–800. By this time, almost every technique known to the Andean weaver had already been invented.**

Opposite: **Handwoven Peruvian textiles and blankets usually have colorful patterns and bright motifs.**

Pottery from the Mochica culture, A.D. 300–1000.

FROM POTTERY TO PAINTING

Some of the earliest remains of visual art in Peru are found in the pottery and weaving of ancient cultures. Many different civilizations, such as the Chavín, Paracas, Nazca, Chimu, and Mochica, developed new techniques and styles that they passed on to the next culture. To this day, the designs and colors from the pottery and textiles of ancient civilizations are used and made in a similar way. Their bright colors make modern masonry and architecture seem dull in comparison. Typical motifs include many fish, reptiles, birds, and mammals. The Mochica culture introduced the representation of everyday human experience: children playing, someone with a toothache, women washing, and lots of portraits.

Military expansion facilitated the spread of artistic styles; with the rise of the Incan empire, its artistic styles became universalized. The Incas incorporated many earlier designs in their work and spread these throughout their empire.

With the coming of the Spanish, painting with oils on canvas and fresco painting were introduced. Churches and monasteries required decorations and paintings: at first these were imported from Spain. Soon European painters arrived, especially from Italy. One of the first was Bernardo Bitti, who emigrated to Peru in 1548.

In the late 19th century, artists began to rediscover their native past. The *costumbrista* (kos-toom-BREE-stah) movement made the everyday life of the native peoples the subject of art. Painters such as José Sebogal tried to create a national school based on native themes.

In the 20th century visual artists were divided into two schools: the *indigenistas* (een-dee-hain-EES-tahs), who follow the native culture and style, and the *hispanistas* (ees-pan-EES-tahs), who draw on the Spanish heritage. Some Peruvian artists have tried to combine the two. Fernando de Szyszlo is the best-known contemporary artist to include native motifs in his abstract painting. Ricardo Grau and Macedonio de la Torre incorporate the traditions of their country with modern European styles.

Peru's most famous modern sculptor, Joaquín Roca Rey, works in metals and has held exhibitions all over the world. His work is exhibited in various museums in the United States and Lima.

THE BRILLIANCE OF INCAN GOLDSMITHS

The quantity of gold that came from Peru in the 16th century was colossal, and most of it was originally in the form of art objects that the Spanish then melted down into ingots. The chronicler Garcilaso de la Vega describes the Emperor Atahualpa's gardens as including life-size imitations of corn,

HUAQUEROS

When the Spanish conquerors plundered the gold of the Incan empire by melting it into bars and sending it back to Spain, they set in motion a practice of robbery that has continued until today. The grave robber is known as a *huaquero* (wah-KAY-roh) after *huaca* (WAH-kah), a temple, burial site, or shrine dating from precolonial times. Archaeologists excavating *huacas* have shown them to be a vital source of information about the Incan way of life. These *huacas* are often characterized by great riches and ornamentation. Temples and the graves of Incan or tribal nobles were often decorated with jewel-encrusted plates of gold that covered whole walls.

The *huaqueros* specialize in finding forgotten *huacas* and then selling the artifacts found inside to the first buyer. These objects frequently end up in European or U.S. private collections. The area around Trujillo is rife with the theft and illegal sale of ancient works of art.

Usually *huaqueros* are very poor people hoping to find and attain huge wealth. Because poverty is widespread in Peru, this is understandable. However, their looting causes great damage, and the archaeologist looking to catalog a *huaca* is inevitably disappointed to find a plundered tomb. Rarely is a *huaca* found intact.

flowers, and animals, all made in gold and silver. Whole buildings and courts were sheathed in plates of gold. Yet nothing, no matter how beautiful, was spared by the Spanish. The examples that survive today are extremely rare and come from remote regions of the Incan empire or from looted graves. Gold was a sacred element. To the Incas it symbolized power and was often used as a tribute to the emperor or buried with nobles. Items buried included images of gods, cups, jewelry, and ornaments.

The tools used to make these objects were primitive, consisting mainly of stone hammers, chisels, and wood and stone rollers for smoothing. Decorative techniques included incising, stamping, scratching, and inlaying with precious metals such as silver and gold, expensive gems such as turquoise and emeralds, as well as amber. The artwork that is preserved in Peru's museums today highlights the astounding craftsmanship and high social standing accorded to craftsworkers in Incan times.

ARCHITECTURE

Before the Incas, buildings were constructed mainly of mud and straw bricks and some wood. Even today many poor people live in mud and straw adobe houses. The artistry of the Incas is visible in their architecture. Incan architecture is technically very accomplished, as can be seen in structures like the walls in Cuzco and the great city of Machu Picchu. Massive blocks of rock were crafted with stone or bronze tools, smoothed off with sand, and then dragged up and down the many steep mountains of Peru using human strength alone. The Incas covered the walls of their dwellings with gold; decorations, statues, and ornaments filled alcoves.

With the arrival of the Spanish, a new style of architecture emerged, which included new types of buildings, such as churches and monasteries. The Spanish relied on native workers and materials, but they created a very Spanish style. Mansions in Lima were replicas of Andalusian structures. Also evident are the Moorish origins of the Spanish style.

Native influences slowly began to seep into architectural style and decorations. Incan motifs, such as the sun and pumas, can often be found in church friezes. Such native touches can be seen in many buildings in the more remote areas, especially Puno and Cajamarca.

One of the most ornate churches in Peru is La Compañía in Cuzco. Its magnificent baroque facade rivals the splendor of the city's cathedral.

MUSIC AND DANCE

Peru's music does not fit into one category. The multitude of different regions, histories, ethnicities, and classes has ensured a wide variety of sounds.

The most famous Peruvian music is the Andean folk music originally played in the highlands. Sad songs are mixed with whooping, energetic ones, and all are performed to a communal and stylized dance.

Andean folk music dates back to the ancient civilizations of Peru. Clay panpipes have been found in ancient graveyards on the coast. The Incas used a variety of flutes and panpipes, conch-shell trumpets, and drums made from puma skin. The Spanish introduced stringed instruments, which the native musicians adapted. Some uniquely Andean instruments used in folk music are the *charrango* (chah-RAHN-go), a kind of mandolin using

Musicians playing in a courtyard. The most popular music in Peru, Andean folk music, is easily found in music halls or *peñas* (PAY-nyahs), especially during festival times.

A rousing folk dance is performed in the highlands. Puno is famous for its traditional folk dances, which are the wildest and most colorfully costumed in the highlands.

an armadillo shell as a sound box, and the Andean harp. Other standard instruments in folk bands are cane flutes, panpipes, and drums.

Peñas, or nightclubs, can be smart and chic or untidy and primitive, but either way they are home to *criolla* (cree-OH-yah), or Creole-style music. Spanish guitars and percussion instruments blend music from many sources, African to European, to create an often slow, romantic form with love ballads. There are regional variations with their own accompanying dances.

Chicha music, named after the beer, developed in Colombia. It is faster than *criolla* and mixes saucy lyrics with energetic percussion and electric guitar backing. *Chicha* can often be heard in the highlands but is heard mainly in the jungle, where it is played at many Saturday night fiestas.

A style that shows the diversity of Peruvian music is *música negra* (MOO-see-kah NAY-grah), or "black music." This style originated in the old slave communities on the coast. The music is associated with social protest and portrays daily life in the communities.

LITERATURE

Peru has provided inspiration to both native and foreign writers. Thornton Wilder wrote The Bridge of San Luis Rey *from an old Peruvian romance he once heard. The fishing villages of Peru's northern coast probably inspired the creation of Ernest Hemingway's* The Old Man and the Sea.

The written word has a relatively recent place in Peruvian history. The Incas had no system of writing, although literature abounded in myths and legends that were passed on orally. The Spanish conquest generated the first pieces of a national literature, mainly historical and descriptive accounts about the conquest. The *Royal Commentaries of the Incas* (1609) is a fascinating document providing many insights into the world of the Incas and the Spanish conquest of Peru. It was written by the Inca Garcilaso de la Vega (not to be confused with the Spanish poet of the same name), who was the son of a conquistador and an Incan princess.

Peruvian writing came into its own only in the past few decades. In previous centuries Peruvian writers had reflected the tastes and forms of Spanish literature. The internationally renowned poet César Vallejo (1892–1938) was one of the first of a generation of poets, artists, and writers to attempt to free himself from European influence and produce a distinct culture, even though he lived abroad for many years. Many of Peru's modern artists, poets, writers, and intellectuals still have to go abroad to discover what is unique about their own country. Through a study of foreign styles, they became more aware of their country's individuality. Vallejo and his contemporaries dealt with themes such as the problems of cultural identity and showed an interest in the Incan heritage.

Peru has also produced good modern novelists in addition to the famous Mario Vargas Llosa. Lesser known but equally important are Ciro Alegría, whose *Broad and Alien Is the World* describes life in the Sierra, and Manuel Scorza, whose *Drums for Runas,* written in the style of the South American magic realist school, deals with the struggles of the miners in the highlands. José María Arguedas was uncommon among Peruvian writers because he wrote solely about the native peoples.

MARIO VARGAS LLOSA—A WRITER IN POLITICS

Mario Vargas Llosa (1936–) is Peru's most famous intellectual and novelist. He first achieved fame in the 1960s when the Mexican Carlos Fuentes and the Colombian Gabriel García Márquez also came to prominence. Like most Latin American writers, Vargas Llosa has also been active in politics.

With over 10 novels, four plays, an abundance of essays, and the first part of his autobiography, *A Fish in the Water*, Vargas Llosa is a prolific author. Born to an affluent family in Arequipa in 1936, he was sent to school at the Military College in Lima at the age of 10. His first novel, *The Time of the Hero*, deals with the effects of the college's cruel and authoritarian regime upon its pupils. The Peruvian military burned the book.

Vargas Llosa is very much a stylist, concentrating on the form and narrative structure of his novels. *Conversations in the Cathedral* is an example of this complexity, a multilayered text profiling corruption and power in the Lima of the 1950s.

Although a native Peruvian, Vargas Llosa had by then spent many years abroad—mostly in Europe—returning only to spend the summer months at his coastal home near Lima. However, he retained a keen interest in Peruvian politics, his views changing as he grew older. Initially holding views of the radical left in the 1960s, he gradually moved to the right. Disagreeing with the nationalization of the banks in 1987, he joined a new right-wing political party called Libertad (Freedom), which later became the Democratic Front. With their help, he began his bid for the presidency, espousing a radical, free-market economic program that would privatize all of Peru's state companies.

The writer who had written so sensitively about his own country was not the politician who entered the 1990 presidential race. Vargas Llosa seemed very remote from the problems of the Peruvian poor. On a second ballot, he was beaten by Alberto Fujimori and flew to London. He became a Spanish citizen and now lives in London.

"Peru is for me a kind of incurable disease and my feeling for her is intense, bitter, and full of the violence that characterizes passion."

—Mario Vargas Llosa

LEISURE

MOST PERUVIANS LEAD A DIFFICULT LIFE, with little time for leisure activities. In the rural areas women may spend leisure moments knitting or doing small tasks around the house. Men may take a leisurely meal or spend some time drinking *chicha*. Otherwise, about the only time to relax is during fiestas, when everyone spends the day (or the week) dancing, eating, and partying.

City dwellers are likely to take a trip to the beach or go to a movie. During the Peruvian summer months of January to April, they flock to seaside resort towns such as Pucusana and La Isla. A favorite pastime is to spend the evening in a *peña*—lively nightclubs with colorful performances—dancing, listening to Creole music, and enjoying drinks and food, such as *ceviche*, a popular seafood. Barranco, a suburb of Lima, is particularly well known for its *peñas*.

Left: **Young people playing volleyball on Uros Island in Lake Titicaca. Peru's women's volleyball team has had great international success.**

Opposite: **Locals relaxing at the Plaza de Armas in southern Arequipa.**

107

A bullfight near Cuzco. Pizarro brought the first fighting bulls to Lima, holding the first bullfight in 1538. Many years later, in 1768, a permanent bullring was built in Lima. It is the third oldest bullring in the world after the ones in Madrid and Seville. Before construction of the bullring, the main town square was used. In rural areas, fields are often used as arenas.

LA CORRIDA DE TOROS

Bullfighting, called *corrida de toros* or the running of the bulls in Peru, is extremely popular with the elite and some of the middle-class Peruvians. Wealthy families breed bulls at their haciendas, encouraging the animals' ferocity and speed, and sponsor fights in Lima. The best matadors are invited from as far afield as Venezuela, Mexico, and Spain and offered as much as $30,000 for an afternoon's sport. The bullfighting season starts in mid-October on the day of the Lord of the Miracles festival and continues until Christmas. There are usually eight fights held each Sunday during this time.

After an opening parade and some initial testing of the bull, the picadors enter on horseback, attacking the bull's shoulders with lances to weaken it. They are followed by the banderilleros, who pierce long darts into the bull's neck to weaken it further. The brightly colored ribbons of the darts flutter as the bull charges around, enraged.

The last act of the drama now begins with the entrance of the matador. The matador maneuvers his muleta, a piece of red cloth fixed to a short stick to tease the bull in preparation for the kill.

After a number of passes, when the matador feels it is time, he kills the bull. The most difficult and dangerous method is *recibiendo* (ray-see-BYEN-doh), where the matador stands directly in front of the bull and thrusts a sword between its horns as it charges. The extreme danger of this technique is heightened by the rule that the matador cannot move his feet until the bull is dead.

The more usual technique is *volapié* (vohl-ah-PYAY), where the matador runs around the agitated and charging bull and stabs it between the shoulder blades. If the kill is successful, the bull dies instantly and the crowd cheers. If it is merely wounded, the crowd may jeer and throw rubbish at the hapless matador.

The occasional matador on horseback distinguishes Peruvian bullfighting from that in other countries. The *paso* horse was developed just for this purpose and is extremely agile in dealing with an unpredictable bull.

At one period in Peruvian bullfighting, the lance and sword were completely dispensed with, leaving the horseman to challenge the agitated bull with just his cape and his courage.

After Mass, churchgoers attend a rural bullfight.

City dwellers, especially in Lima, like nothing better on the weekend than a trip to the beach.

SPORTS

Sports have always been a good way of bringing a community together, and in small villages, the reward after a hard day's work is often found in playing on the local soccer team. Sports have been popular since early times. The Incas played versions of badminton and basketball, which were illustrated on ancient vases.

Soccer is the favorite sport in Peru today, although there are also baseball and basketball teams. Pool and tenpin bowling are also played. Many country clubs offer golf, swimming, and tennis. Volleyball and polo also have a large following (the women's volleyball team won a silver medal at the 1982 Olympics), and even the English game of cricket is played at the Lima Cricket Club. However, these are the sports for the rich. Recreation facilities for everyone are more plentiful in the cities than in the country. Recently volleyball, which is enjoyed by the masses, has been increasing in popularity, and the Peruvian team will take part in the next Olympics in Beijing, China, in 2008.

WATER SPORTS

The village of Ancón, north of Lima, was an old fishing village that, for a period, became a playground for the wealthy, who would go there to fish and sail. The Cano Blanco was a famous and exclusive fishing club in the village that counted Ernest Hemingway among its visitors. Yachting is a popular pastime today, even for lower-income Peruvians, with many sailing to the Galapagos Islands. Deep-sea fishing is popular all along the western coast, where the catch includes black marlin, flounder, sea bass, snook, corvina, and mackerel. In the Andean lakes, fly-fishing for trout is extremely popular, and many tourists come from Europe and the United States to try their luck.

BEACHES

The most fashionable and famous beaches lie south of Lima. Their vibrant nightlife makes them the favorite haunts of young Peruvians. Daytime activities include yachting and surfing.

SOCCER

Soccer, called *fútbol*, is the most popular sport in Peru. The National Stadium in Lima hosts the most important soccer matches and events. The national team qualified for the 1982 World Cup in Spain but failed to qualify in 1994.

Soccer was first played in Lima in 1892. It was introduced by British immigrants, and the first club was founded in 1897, with leagues starting in 1912. A tragic incident in May 1964 highlights the seriousness with which the sport is taken. Nearly 300 people were killed when riots broke out in Lima after Argentina scored a last-minute winning goal against Peru.

Watching cockfights is a favorite pastime in Peru.

HORSE RACING

Horse racing is a popular spectator sport, and races are held most weekends and some weekday evenings in the summer. Peruvian horse racing takes place at Lima's hippodrome on most evenings except Mondays. Racing is mainly for the moderately wealthy and town dwellers. Each April, Lima's National Concourse celebrates Peru's famous pacing horses, with high society coming to watch dressage competitions.

COCKFIGHTING

Cockfighting, which is illegal in most of the United States, is very much the spectator sport of choice among the poor. Trained cocks are placed face to face in a pit or on a stage and let loose to fight each other. The birds are fitted with sharp spurs on their legs, which they use to attack the opponent until one is killed or becomes unable to fight. There are three types of cockfights: the single battle in which two cocks fight; the main battle, where cocks are paired and play an elimination game; and the battle royal, in which several cocks fight each other until only one is standing. The Coliseo de Gallos in Lima hosts fights on most weekends.

SAPO

Sapo is a popular local game in Peru that is played in *picanterías* (pee-kahn-tuh-REE-ahs), or small local restaurants, and is as common as pool in the United States. *Sapo* means frog, and the game uses a large metal frog mounted on a table. Players throw brass discs as close to the frog as possible. The highest score is obtained when the disc is thrown into the frog's open mouth. Men can spend the whole afternoon, and evening, drinking *chicha* and competing in this old game.

MOUNTAINEERING AND HIKING

The Andes was an impassable problem rather than a source of pleasure until the start of the 20th century, when climbing and hiking through the rugged mountains became a popular pastime. More than 30 peaks rise well above 20,000 feet (6,096 m) in a region that can only be compared with the Himalayas. The most beautiful views are found by climbing the Cordillera Blanca. Mountaineering in this area is strictly for the adventurous because of the obvious danger and the problem of high-altitude sickness.

Hikers along the Incan trail can wander along paths that have been used for centuries, although they may have to make room for herds of goats or llamas.

FESTIVALS

THE WORD *FIESTA* is Spanish for feast and is usually a holiday associated with the celebration of a religious event. Fiestas are often accompanied by dancing, feasting, and music. Church bells ring, fireworks explode, processions begin and end, and eating and drinking never stop. Beneath all this gaiety there is sometimes a serious reason for the festival.

Today fiestas are held not only to commemorate religious events but also to mark ethnic-specific or national occasions. Those connected with national celebrations are more somber.

The most important national holidays are the Day of National Honor on October 9 and the Independence Days on July 28–29. They are occasions for speeches and military parades and a chance for local politicians to campaign for upcoming elections.

Church festivals, on the other hand, are bright, colorful, energetic events, and far more popular. The Holy Week processions at Ayacucho attract people from all over the world.

The fiesta is an opportunity to bring color and laughter into lives that are often a hard struggle for existence. Whether the celebration is wholly Christian, partly native, or a blend of African, Spanish, and Incan rituals, the fiesta is there to be enjoyed by everyone.

Each festival occurs only once a year, and because of this, it is eagerly awaited and anticipated by all. It is a day for the whole community to take part in and look forward to, a day when the poverty and hard work of everyday life are momentarily forgotten. It is therefore not surprising that each festival is celebrated in such high spirits.

Above: **The Corpus Cristi Festival in Cuzco.**

Opposite: **Girls performing a mestizo dance. This dance has European influences and is popular during local festivities and celebrations of patron saints.**

115

COMMUNITY FIESTAS

Nearly every community has its own saint or patron figure, who is often very significant to local people. In the mountains and in small villages, their particular patron saint's day is both a splendid occasion and a well-earned holiday. The early Spanish missionaries, who were eager to get rid of the Incan religion, chose a saint's day that coincided with the most important pagan festival in each village, town, and city. This enabled them to change the pagan festival into an event of Christian significance.

CALENDAR OF FESTIVALS

January 1	New Year's Day	June 29	Saints Peter and
January 6	Epiphany		Paul's Day
February	(First two weeks)	July 28–29	Independence Days
	Candlemas Festival Fiesta	August 15	Feast of the Assumption
	de la Virgen de la	August 30	Saint Rose of Lima,
	Candelaria (Puno)		patron saint of Peru
February/March	Carnival	October 8	Battle of Angamos Day
March/April	Maundy Thursday, Good	October 18	Lord of the Miracles in
	Friday, Easter		Lima
May 1	Labor Day	November 1	All Saints' Day
June	(Ninth Thursday after Easter)	December 8	Feast of the Immaculate
	Corpus Cristi		Conception
June 24	Inti Raymi in Cuzco Day	December 25	Christmas

A special type of fiesta is known as the *feria* (FAY-ree-ah), which means fair or market in Spanish. The *feria* usually falls on a weekday when no festival occurs. There is a solemn reason for feast days, but the *feria* is mainly for entertainment, although masses are often said.

Religious festivals generally include a great fair or market, as well as fireworks, bullfights, communal dancing with the people in traditional dress, roast pig, and lots of *chicha*. Special masses are often said, sometimes combined with a procession that includes carrying a saint's statue or other holy images. Market days frequently coincide with fiestas, allowing local vendors to sell their wares to a large crowd.

Some of the most elaborate and colorful festivals are those belonging to the native peoples and the minority groups of blacks, Chinese, and Japanese who populate Peru. The September fiesta in Trujillo combines Andalusian, African, and native music with skillful dancing. These dances are performed in *peñas* all over the country, but rarely are they performed as well as they are in Trujillo.

Above: **Dancing at the September festival in Chincheros. Folk dancing, besides be-ing a social entertainment, is a way of bringing the community together, both young and old, women and men.**

Opposite: **A village festival in the highlands. Festivals range from elaborate to very simple.**

Priests leading the Corpus Cristi procession in Cuzco.

FIESTAS IN CUZCO

Cuzco has an important fiesta occurring nearly every month. One of the oldest fiestas originated on March 31, 1650, when Cuzco was shattered by a major earthquake. A small statue known as *Nuestro Señor de los Temblores* (NWAY-stro say-NYOR day los taym-BLOH-rays), or "Our Lord of the Earthquakes," was taken out and paraded around the city. The people believed this saved them from further destruction. Every year since then, on the first Monday of Holy Week, this statue of Christ, known to the natives as *Taitacha* (tye-TAH-chah), meaning "Little Father," is carried on a three-hour circuit of Cuzco.

Corpus Cristi occurs on the Thursday after Trinity Sunday. The day before this, 13 statues of saints are taken from their respective churches in the suburbs or barrios of Cuzco. They are paraded on enormous litters, each carried by 20 to 40 men and led by brass bands and parishioners who carry banners and candles and are followed by praying devotees. On Corpus Cristi, the Plaza de Armas is filled with the faithful, some of whom come hundreds of miles to be there. Large altars decorated with flowers, mirrors, crosses—and images of the sun, remnants of Incan heritage—are erected on three sides of the plaza.

June is the climax of the festival season in Cuzco, with two important Incan and church festivals: Inti Raymi and Corpus Cristi.

118

After High Mass the statues are paraded around the plaza on their litters until each has "bowed" to all the others. These litters can weigh up to a ton because of their gold and silver decorations. The litter is followed by other parishioners in brightly colored festival clothes and by musicians. Sometimes old women sing hymns in Quechua.

CARNIVAL

Carnavales (kar-nah-VAH-lays) is a great, joyous explosion celebrated throughout Peru. The word *carnival* comes from the Latin *carne vale*, which means "farewell to the flesh." Carnival is the last opportunity for people to drink, dance, and be merry before the fasting period of Lent.

The Quechua term for Carnavales is *jatum pujllay* (ja-TUM POOJ-lay), or "the great game." This originates from the native tradition of rounding up wild game for presentation to the parish priest and the mayor, who in return provided *chicha* and coca leaves. Today, because game is less plentiful, lambs and farm animals are usually offered. The offering of the animals is a fertility rite going back to Incan days, when the Incas gave offerings and sacrifices to their gods in anticipation of a good harvest. The idea of fertility survives today, as Carnival is still regarded by many as the best opportunity for meeting or courting future husbands and wives.

Corpus Cristi in Cuzco. The litters are carried by the parishioners of the church to which the statue belongs. It is regarded as a great honor to be a litter bearer.

Above: **An actor playing the role of an Incan emperor is brought in for an Inti Raymi celebration.**

Opposite: **Musicians in traditional dress at an Inti Raymi celebration.**

INTI RAYMI

Inti Raymi (Father Sun) or Festival of the Sun, on June 24, is the Incan celebration of the winter solstice, when the sun is farthest from the earth, and is dedicated to prayers for the return of the sun. The Incas believed that the sun regulates the universe and controls the lives of plants, animals, and people. Many modern natives still believe that the sun and moon are gods capable of punishing or helping people.

Because the saint's day for Saint John the Baptist falls on June 24, the Spanish simply converted the ancient festival into a Christian one. Remnants of the original Incan festival still survive: fires left burning throughout the night of June 23 are not in praise of Saint John, but to bring back the sun after the longest night of the year.

The Inti Raymi of today was recreated in the 1940s based on eyewitness reports that the early colonists recorded. Before the ceremony someone is chosen to be emperor of all the Incas and is carried into Sacsayhuamán fortress on a litter. The emperor has a palace guard (composed of members of the Peruvian army in Incan costume) and traditionally dressed dancers who dance before him, recreating an ancient battle that ended in victory. The pageant begins with a ceremonial relighting of the fires, which is symbolic of the return of the emperor and the Incas. People also burn their old clothes to symbolize an end to poverty, while marking the year's harvest and the beginning of the new year. A llama is sacrificed to the sun (but not killed), and the music and dancing go on for three hours. For the rest of the week the city celebrates.

DANCERS OF THE DEVIL IN PUNO

The department of Puno is located in the densely populated, poor, and southernmost part of Peru, bordering Lake Titicaca and Bolivia. It is the folk center of Peru and boasts a wide range of handicrafts, legends, costumes, and dances. Over 300 ethnic dances are performed there, some of which are rarely seen by outsiders. The dances are usually reserved for the annual fiestas, especially church festivals, although they date from preconquest days. Many of them revolve around the agricultural life of the people and celebrate planting and harvest times.

Although most of the dances are complex, what is most apparent is the dancers' elaborately embroidered costumes. These are extremely rich and ornate and are often the most expensive single item the family owns. Besides traditional indigenous atttire with bowler hats and whirling skirts, the costumes also include grotesque masks, sequined uniforms, and animal costumes—all in bright colors.

The native peoples in this part of the world are accustomed to great hardship, and thus they celebrate their few holidays with great enthusiasm. During the feast of the Virgin of Candelaria, or Candelmas, the Dance of the Devil can be seen. Masks are worn by the dancers, who compete fiercely to outdance each other in the *Diablada* (dee-ah-BLAH-dah), which symbolizes the victory of good over evil. The dancers gesticulate and contort their bodies into horrible positions and frighten the children. This dance probably dates back to pre-Incan civilizations.

FOOD

PERU'S VARIED CLIMATE AND GEOGRAPHY have produced the most extensive and assorted menu in South America. Besides geographic differences, there are also variations in the diets of the rich and the poor: the poor eat much like the ancient Incas, with corn, peppers, and potatoes being important staples; the rich enjoy a blend of native and European cooking that has evolved into the style of cuisine known as *criolla* (cree-OH-yah), or Creole.

Specializing in spicy food, modern Peru has many local delicacies ranging from seafood on the coast to old Incan recipes such as roast guinea pig in peanut sauce. But the staples on which most of the population survive are still peppers, potatoes, and grains.

The ancient civilizations showed the primary cultural importance that food had in the community in their pottery and weaving. For example, priests in pre-Incan societies decided the times for planting based on their astral predictions.

Ancient peoples would often bury food with their dead, believing that that would help to sustain them on their journey to the next life. The Aymará around Lake Titicaca still stuff coca leaves in potatoes and bury them as a sacrifice to the earth mother, Pachamama.

Left: **The Sunday vegetable market in the main square of Pisac.**

Opposite: **Peruvians cook a traditional soup called puchero during La Porciuncula at the convent of Los Descalzos, in Lima. La Porciuncula is a religious activity where Franciscan priests give food to poor people.**

An Aymará family enjoying a banquet of potatoes. Potatoes, or papas, are the mainstay of the Peruvian diet, although they are often regarded as the food of the poor.

Even today, new varieties of potatoes are being discovered and exported. These new exports include the yellow Limeña potato, the olluco, which ranges in color from red, pink, and orange to white, and a potato with purple skin that encases an equally purple potato within.

POTATOES, CORN, AND PEPPERS

Because the coast is too arid to grow many crops and the Amazon jungle is too densely forested to be cultivated, the majority of the crops come from the highlands. Potatoes are indigenous to the Andes and were exported from the highland regions to Europe and the rest of the Americas beginning in the 16th century. There are over 200 varieties, some completely unknown outside the Andes. A farmer with a small plot of land may plant up to three dozen different varieties in one field.

Some potatoes grow at over 8,000 feet (2,450 m) having adapted to that height and become frost resistant. People in the highlands freeze-dry their potato crop to ensure that food is available later in the season. The potatoes are frozen on the ground at night when the temperature is below zero and then thawed out the next day as the sun warms the air; they are then frozen again that night. This process continues until they are completely dehydrated. The potato becomes dry and cardboardlike. It is then stored and can be kept for up to four years. These potatoes, called *chúo* (choonyo) and *moraya* (more-I-ya), are popular in stews in the Andeas, where they are cooked like any other vegetable.

Corn comes in as many varieties as the potato and was regarded as sacred by the pre-Hispanic peoples. It was used for bartering and as a form of currency, as well as for food.

Hot peppers, found in many varieties, are lavishly used in everything from fish to soups. Marketplaces become a dazzling display of color as enormous baskets full of peppers in sun-yellow, flaming orange, fiery red, and bright green are sold and bought. On the coast, where fish is common in the diet, sauces of onions and peppers are served in side bowls as condiments or heaped straight onto the meal. In the Amazon area, food is a little less spicy, but people there still dip vegetables in pepper sauces. It is in the highland areas that the *picante* (pee-KAHN-tay) or spicy form of cooking reaches an art form. Dishes are often laid out in degrees of spiciness according to the chili pepper used, ranging from bland to volcanic.

Different varieties of corn. Purple corn is traditionally used to make chicha. Another type of chicha, a thick white variety, is poured on the earth during harvest and planting rituals in the highlands.

It is believed that South American natives originally grew five different types of pepper, which gradually traveled to Central America, Mexico, and the Caribbean. They were mistakenly called peppers by early Spanish explorers looking for black pepper. They found the natives were accustomed to eating peppers at every meal and soon began to export them to Europe, Africa, and Asia. In India peppers became a staple in cooking.

A standard lunch includes chicken soup, meat, rice, and a drink.

Fish is believed to have rejuvenating powers. A thick rice and fish soup (aguadito) is traditionally served to all-night partygoers. Signs on street stalls often tout the aguadito's energy-boosting properties.

TRADITIONAL CUISINE

Local dishes are often called *criolla*, or Creole, meaning they are a mixture of Spanish and indigenous cuisines. *A la criolla* also refers to spicy foods. Many cultures have contributed to Peruvian cuisine: black slaves from the West Indies and Africa, Polynesian slaves from the Pacific Islands, Chinese and Japanese immigrants, and, of course, Spanish and native peoples.

Piqueo (pee-KAY-oh), or appetizers, are a specialty of Peru. The servings are frequently so large that there is little room for the main course.

A favorite *piqueo* is Arequipa-style potatoes, or *Ocopas Arequipeña*. These are potatoes boiled, sliced, and served with a peanut, cheese, and chili sauce. Most appetizers are dips, and you can have many varieties at one sitting.

There are also unusual Peruvian dishes. *Anticuchos* (an-tee-KOO-chohs) are skewers of beef heart with hot peppers and seasoning barbecued over glowing coals. This dish is usually available from street vendors.

Another unusual speciality is *causa a la Limeña* (COW-sah ah lah lee-MAY-nyah), made from yellow potatoes, olives, onions, boiled eggs, peppers, prawns, and cheese.

Smoked fish is popular, especially smoked trout from the highlands. In the Pachamanca style of cooking, meat and frequently fish are cooked by wrapping them in leaves, usually banana, and steaming them beneath layers of earth and charcoal.

One of the best desserts is *mazamorra morada* (mah-zah-MOH-rah moh-RAH-dah), which is a sweet casserole made from pineapples, peaches, apples, dried fruit, quinces, sugar, and purple corn. It is served hot and sprinkled with cinnamon.

REGIONAL DELICACIES

Authentic Peruvian cuisine is more likely to be served in the highlands. Dishes include *rocoto relleno* (roh-COH-toh ray-YAY-noh), spicy bell peppers stuffed with ground beef and vegetables; *chicharrones* (chee-chah-ROH-nays), deep-fried chunks of pork rib called *chancho* or chicken called *gallina*; *choclo con queso* (CHOH-cloh kon KAY-so), corn on the cob with cheese; and the obligatory *tamales*, cornmeal and meat or beans wrapped in corn husks.

In the Amazon basin, people eat *farina,* a dish made from yucca, a plant similar to the potato. This is eaten fried or mixed with lemonade. In the markets, children sell hot *pan de arroz* (pahn day ah-ROHZ), a bread made from rice flour, yucca, and butter that takes three days to prepare. Some regional specialities include *juanes* (HWAH nays), which is fish or chicken steamed in a banana leaf with rice or yucca, and *chocann* (CHOH-can), a soup of fish chunks flavored with cilantro. Fish dishes are popular, and the Amazon River provides everything from the small flesh-eating piranhas to the huge *paiches* (PIE-chays).

On the coast and in the desert regions, food is prepared in the same hearty manner as in the highlands, but with fish, chicken, or goat instead of beef. A favorite dish is roast kid cooked with *chicha* and served with beans and rice. But the best coastal dishes are those containing seafood. *Ceviche,* or marinated whitefish, is the most traditional.

Grains such as the purple-flowered kiwacha *and golden-brown* quinoa *disappeared for centuries under Spanish rule. They were used in Incan ceremonies, and when the Catholic Church banned the Incan religion, they also banned the grains. Besides taking away a part of their culture, the Spanish also took away a nourishing food source that is high in protein. Today native peoples are using these grains again.*

DINING OUT

In most villages local restaurants called *picanterías* (literally "spicy places" because of the use of peppers) or quintas, country houses, serve typical dishes of the area. Most of the *picanterías* are open only two or three days a week, but because there are so many, one at least is always open. Live music is often played, and they are the social center of many communities. Quintas provide the same service in the suburbs.

Another popular type of restaurant and one that shows Peru's ethnic diversity is the *chifas* (CHEE-fahs), or Chinese restaurants, that dot the coastal towns, making noodles part of the staple diet in some parts of Peru. Of a more basic nature are taverns called *chicherías* (chee-cha-REE-ahs), named after the Andean speciality *chicha*, the corn beer. They also serve meals and snacks.

Peruvian streets are often filled with vendors selling shish kebabs and fish—in fact, anything that is portable and edible. Generally, Peruvians have a very sweet tooth and indulge in the many desserts sold on the streets, like *churro* (CHOO-roh), a deep-fried tube of pastry filled with custard or, in the summer, cones of crushed ice flavored with fruit syrups, which are available on virtually every street corner.

The gold-colored Inca Kola is a popular soft drink among Peruvians.

DRINKS

Tap water in South America is not completely safe. Although it may come from a chlorination or filtration plant, the pipes that carry it to the tap are usually old, cracked, or contain dirt. Only the elite and middle class drink bottled water, frequently the carbonated kind.

PERUVIANS' PET DISH—GUINEA PIG

In most parts of the world, guinea pigs are kept as pets. In Peru, however, the cuddly companion is a staple food for the locals. About 65 million guinea pigs are consumed in Peru every year—often fried, roasted, or grilled over charcoal, and eaten with rice, potatoes, and salad. Said to taste like rabbit, it is also served in a stew in which the meat is marinated in beer before being cooked.

This well-loved Peruvian dish, known as *cuy*, dates back to Incan times, when the commoners would dry out guinea pig skin, and use it in soups and stews. Every July the Incas would sacrifice 1,000 guinea pigs along with 100 llamas, to protect their crops from droughts and floods. Since then, farmers have bred the rodents for food. They are a vital source of protein for rural dwellers, and are used in traditional Andean medicine. *Curanderos* or spiritual healers still use them to diagnose illnesses.

In 2004 Peruvian scientists introduced a new breed of "super" guinea pig, which is almost twice the normal size at 2.5 pounds (1.1 kg). Low in fat and cholesterol, it took over 30 years to develop and is said to be meatier, tastier, and richer in protein than its precursor. Up to 1,000 of these are exported weekly to the United States, Japan, and Europe, catering largely to the Peruvian expatriate and immigrant communities.

Tea is usually served with lemon and sugar. Peru grows its own coffee, but its coffee lacks the excellence of that grown in neighboring Colombia. A traditional method of making coffee is to boil it for hours until only a thick, dark syrup, called *essencia* remains. This is poured into cruets, which are small glass bottles used for holding liquids, and diluted with hot milk or water. Nowadays instant coffee mix is more common.

Besides many of the usual varieties of soft drinks, or *gaseosas* (gah-say-OH-sas), sold in the United States, Peru also has its own varieties, which are very sweet. A local favorite is Inca Kola, a gold colored soda. Fruit juices are common and come in many exotic flavors: blackberry, passion fruit, and watermelon, to name but a few.

Most adults, especially in rural areas, drink *chicha*. This beer is made by fermenting corn or quinoa (a plant with starchy seeds). Its thick, off-white appearance looks like soup and the taste is acquired. Some of the recipes date back to the Incas. A red or white bunch of flowers or a plastic bag on a pole is left outside a house to indicate that *chicha* is for sale there. Peru's national drink, *pisco*, a clear wine made of white grapes, gets its name from the city of Pisco in southern Peru.

In the Andes, cooking is more difficult. Air exerts less pressure at high altitudes, and recipes have to be adjusted. The change in altitude mostly affects foods that require baking or boiling or those that contain a lot of sugar.

AJI DE GALLINA (CHICKEN IN SPICY SAUCE)

This recipe serves four people.

1 whole chicken (about 4 pounds/2 kg)
1 medium onion, chopped
1 carrot, chopped
1 celery stalk, chopped
Bouquet garni (3 stalks parsley, 1 sprig thyme, and
2 bay leaves, tied together with a piece of string)
Salt and freshly ground pepper
3 slices of white bread, crusts removed
½ cup (4 ounces/120 ml) olive oil
2 cups (10 ounces/285 g) red onion, finely chopped
4 cloves garlic, minced
½ teaspoon dried oregano
1 teaspoon ground cumin
1½ cups (16 ounces/450 g) *ají amarillo* paste (yellow chili pepper)
2 tablespoons *ají mirasol* paste (brown chili pepper)
(Both pastes are available ready-made in jars from markets and specialty food stores)
3 tablespoons grated Parmesan cheese
3 tablespoons walnuts, finely chopped
1½ cups (12 ounces/355 ml) evaporated milk
Small potatoes, boiled, peeled, and halved
2–3 hard-cooked eggs, sliced

Add enough water to cover the chicken in a large pot, then add the medium onion, carrot, celery, bouquet garni, and salt. Cover and bring to a boil. Reduce heat and simmer until the chicken is tender. Remove the chicken and cool for a few minutes. Pull the meat from the bones, shred into bite-size pieces, and discard the skin. Strain the broth and discard the vegetables. Set aside. Soak the bread in 1 cup (8 fl ounces/250 ml) of the broth for a few minutes. Place the bread mixture in a blender and puree until smooth.

Heat the oil in a large pan, and sauté the red onions and garlic until soft and golden. Add oregano, cumin, *ají amarillo* paste, *ají mirasol* paste, salt, and freshly ground pepper. Stir for a few minutes. Add the bread mixture and cook for 2 minutes. Add 2 cups (16 fl ounces/500 ml) of broth and the chicken pieces. Stir in Parmesan cheese and walnuts, and simmer gently for 5 minutes. Add evaporated milk before serving and stir thoroughly. Serve with rice or potatoes and hard-cooked eggs. Garnish with bits of chopped walnuts, chopped parsley, and black olives.

ALFAJORES (CARAMEL SANDWICH COOKIES)

This recipe makes 24 cookies.

For the dough

1½ cups (12 ounces/340 g) unsalted butter
1 cup (4 ounces/115 g) confectioners' sugar
2 tablespoons granulated sugar
¼ teaspoon salt
¼ teaspoon almond extract
½ teaspoon vanilla extract
⅓ cup (1 ounce/30 g) ground almonds (can be ground in a food processor)
3 cups (4½ ounces/130 g) all-purpose flour

For the filling

2 cups (14 ounces/400 g) brown sugar
2 cans (14 ounces/395 g)
sweetened condensed milk
3 tablespoons unsalted butter
½ teaspoon vanilla extract

To make the dough, beat together the butter and sugar in a large bowl until light and fluffy. Add salt, almond and vanilla extracts, ground almonds, and flour, mixing well. Stir until the dough can be rolled. Knead the dough lightly until it is smooth. Chill for 30 minutes.

For the filling, heat the brown sugar with condensed milk over medium heat in a saucepan. Keep stirring until the milk thickens and becomes brown. Remove from heat and let it cool. Stir in butter and beat until mixture is thickened. Add vanilla. (If too thick, heat to loosen or add more milk.) If the mixture is too thin, add more confectioners' sugar.

To make the cookies, roll out the chilled dough on a floured work surface to ½-inch (1 cm) thickness and cut into 2½-inch (6-cm) circles. Place on a greased and floured cookie sheet, and bake at 350°F (180°C) for about 12 to 14 minutes. Be careful not to let them brown at all. Transfer to a rack and cool for about 10 minutes.

Spread some caramel filling on a cookie. Top with another cookie and press together carefully. Dust confectioners' sugar over tops of cookies.

A B C D

Equator

ECUADOR **COLOMBIA**

1

● Capital city
● Major town
▲ Mountain peak
■ Ancient site

Feet   Meters
16,500   5,000
9,900   3,000
6,600   2,000
3,300   1,000
1,650   500
660   200
0   0

Tigre

Iquitos ●
L O R E T O

Amazon

Nauta ●

TUMBES

Talara ●

Sullana ●

Piura ● Chulucanas ●

2 **PIURA**

Marañón

Huallaga

Ucayali

B R A Z I L

N

LAMBAYEQUE

Chiclayo ●

Cajamarca ●

Chan Chan ■ **SAN**
MARTÍN

Trujillo ● **LA**
LIBERTAD

CAJAMARCA

AMAZONAS

Mount Huascarán
(22,205 ft / 6,765 m)

Chimbote ● ▲ **HUÁNUCO**

3 **ANCASH** Huánuco ●

UCAYALI

PASCO

Urubamba

*P
e
r
u

C
u
r
r
e
n
t*

JUNÍN

MADRE DE
DIOS

Callao ● **LIMA**

Huancayo ● *Madre de Dios*

● LIMA

HUANCAVELICA

Apurímac

Machu Picchu
Ruins

4 ■ **CUZCO**

Chincha
Island

Pisco ● **APURIMAC**

Chincheros ● ● Cuzco

ICA **AYACUCHO**

Nazca ●

PUNO

Lake
Titicaca

AREQUIPA *El Misti*

Arequipa ● ▲ Puno ●

BOLIVIA

P A C I F I C

O C E A N

Matarani ●

5 Mollendo ● **MOQUEGUA**

TACNA

Tacna ●

CHILE

MAP OF PERU

Amazon (river), C2

Ancash (region), A3–B3

Apurimac (region), B4–C4

Arequipa, C5

Ayacucho (region), B4–B5, C4–C5

Bolivia, C4–C5, D3–D5

Brazil, C2–C4, D1–D4

Cajamarca, A3

Callao, B4

Chan Chan, A3

Chiclayo, A2

Chile, C5–D5

Chimbote, A3

Chincheros, B4

Chincha Island, B4

Chulucanas, A2

Colombia, B1, C1–C2

Cuzco, C4

Ecuador, A1–A2, B1

El Misti, C5

Huancavelica (region), B4

Huancayo, B4

Huánuco (region), B3

Ica (region), B4

Iquitos, C2

Junín (region), B3–B4, C4

La Libertad (region), A3–B3

Lake Titicaca, C5

Lima, B4

Machu Picchu Ruins, C4

Madre de Dios (region), C3–C4

Marañón (river), B2

Matarani, C5

Mollendo, C5

Mount Huascarán, B3

Nauta (city), C2

Nazca, B4

Pasco (region), B3–B4

Pisco, B4

Piura, A2

Puno, C5

Sullana, A2

Tacna, C5

Talara, A2

Tigre (river), B1–B2

Trujillo, A3

Urubamba (river), C3–C4

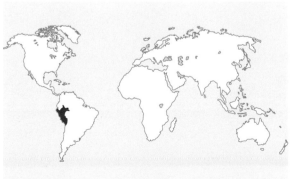

ECONOMIC PERU

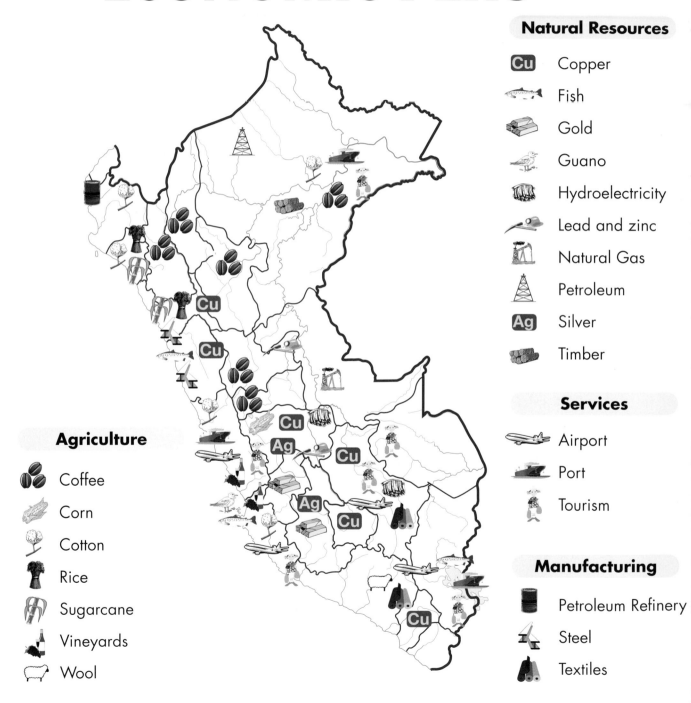

Natural Resources

Cu   Copper
Fish
Gold
Guano
Hydroelectricity
Lead and zinc
Natural Gas
Petroleum
Ag   Silver
Timber

Services

Airport
Port
Tourism

Manufacturing

Petroleum Refinery
Steel
Textiles

Agriculture

Coffee
Corn
Cotton
Rice
Sugarcane
Vineyards
Wool

ABOUT THE ECONOMY

GROSS DOMESTIC PRODUCT (GDP)
$78.2 billion (2005 estimate)

GDP GROWTH
6.6 percent (2005 estimate)

GDP BY SECTORS
Services 65 percent; industry 27 percent; agriculture 8 percent (2003 estimate)

GDP PER CAPITA
$2,798 (2005 estimate)

INFLATION RATE
1.6 percent (2005 estimate)

NATURAL RESOURCES
Iron, copper, gold, silver, zinc, lead, fish, petroleum, natural gas, timber, coal, phosphate, potash, hydropower

AGRICULTURAL PRODUCTS
Coffee, cotton, sugarcane, potato, rice, bananas, poultry, milk, corn, grapes, oranges, coca, cocoa

CULTIVATED LAND
3.2 million acres (1.3 million ha)

CURRENCY
Nuevo sol
USD 1 = 3.3 nuevos soles (2005 estimate)

MAIN EXPORTS
Gold, copper, fish meal, zinc, oil, lead, coffee, petroleum, textiles, asparagus, apparel

MAIN IMPORTS
Machinery, vehicles, processed food, petroleum

MAJOR EXPORT MARKETS
United States 29 percent, China 9.9 percent, United Kingdom 9.1 percent, Chile 5.9 percent, Japan 4.4 percent, others 41.7 percent (2004 estimates)

MAJOR IMPORT SUPPLIERS
United States 19.6 percent, Colombia 7.7 percent, China 7.6 percent, Spain 7.4 percent, Brazil and Venezuela 6.9 percent, and others 50.8 percent (2004 estimates)

LABOR FORCE
11 million (2004 estimate)

LABOR FORCE BY SECTOR
Services 73 percent, industry 18 percent, agriculture 9 percent (2003 estimates)

UNEMPLOYMENT RATE
8.4 percent (2005 estimate)

POPULATION BELOW POVERTY LINE
54 percent (2003 estimate)

TOURISM REVENUE
Over $1 billion annually

TRADE BALANCE
$241 million (2005 estimate)

CULTURAL PERU

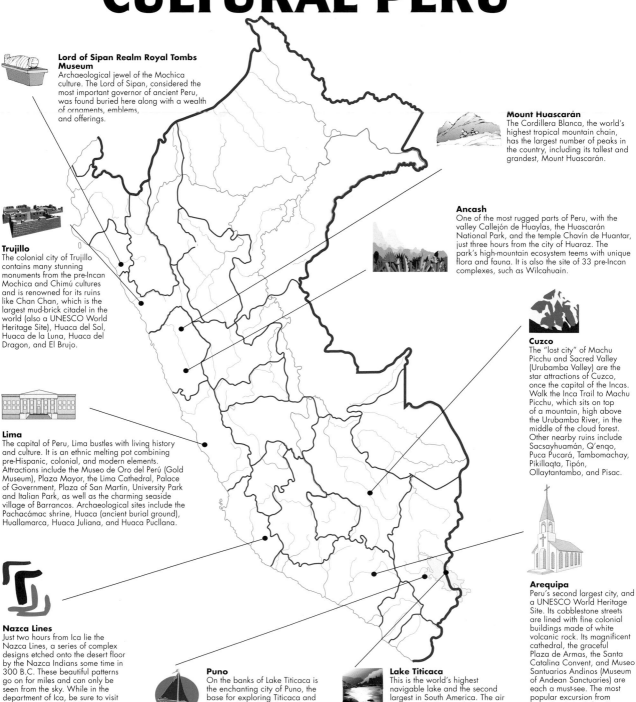

Lord of Sipan Realm Royal Tombs Museum
Archaeological jewel of the Mochica culture. The Lord of Sipan, considered the most important governor of ancient Peru, was found buried here along with a wealth of ornaments, emblems, and offerings.

Mount Huascarán
The Cordillera Blanca, the world's highest tropical mountain chain, has the largest number of peaks in the country, including its tallest and grandest, Mount Huascarán.

Ancash
One of the most rugged parts of Peru, with the valley Callejón de Huaylas, the Huascarán National Park, and the temple Chavín de Huantar, just three hours from the city of Huaraz. The park's high-mountain ecosystem teems with unique flora and fauna. It is also the site of 33 pre-Incan complexes, such as Wilcahuain.

Trujillo
The colonial city of Trujillo contains many stunning monuments from the pre-Incan Mochica and Chimú cultures and is renowned for its ruins like Chan Chan, which is the largest mud-brick citadel in the world (also a UNESCO World Heritage Site), Huaca del Sol, Huaca de la Luna, Huaca del Dragon, and El Brujo.

Cuzco
The "lost city" of Machu Picchu and Sacred Valley (Urubamba Valley) are the star attractions of Cuzco, once the capital of the Incas. Walk the Inca Trail to Machu Picchu, which sits on top of a mountain, high above the Urubamba River, in the middle of the cloud forest. Other nearby ruins include Sacsayhuamán, Q'enqo, Puca Pucará, Tambomachay, Pikillaqta, Tipón, Ollaytantambo, and Pisac.

Lima
The capital of Peru, Lima bustles with living history and culture. It is an ethnic melting pot combining pre-Hispanic, colonial, and modern elements. Attractions include the Museo de Oro del Perú (Gold Museum), Plaza Mayor, the Lima Cathedral, Palace of Government, Plaza of San Martín, University Park and Italian Park, as well as the charming seaside village of Barrancos. Archaeological sites include the Pachacámac shrine, Huaca (ancient burial ground), Huallamarca, Huaca Juliana, and Huaca Pucllana.

Arequipa
Peru's second largest city, and a UNESCO World Heritage Site. Its cobblestone streets are lined with fine colonial buildings made of white volcanic rock. Its magnificent cathedral, the graceful Plaza de Armas, the Santa Catalina Convent, and Museo Santuarios Andinos (Museum of Andean Sanctuaries) are each a must-see. The most popular excursion from Arequipa is to Colca Canyon, the world's deepest canyon.

Nazca Lines
Just two hours from Ica lie the Nazca Lines, a series of complex designs etched onto the desert floor by the Nazca Indians some time in 300 B.C. These beautiful patterns go on for miles and can only be seen from the sky. While in the department of Ica, be sure to visit the Paracas National Reserve, the only protected area in Peru that includes a marine ecosystem.

Puno
On the banks of Lake Titicaca is the enchanting city of Puno, the base for exploring Titicaca and its many islands by boat, the Aymará inhabitants, and colorful folk traditions.

Lake Titicaca
This is the world's highest navigable lake and the second largest in South America. The air is unusually clear and the azure waters particularly striking.

ABOUT THE CULTURE

OFFICIAL NAME
Republic of Peru

NATIONAL FLAG
Three vertical red-white-red stripes, with a coat of arms in the middle. This contains a shield featuring a vicuña, a cinchona tree, and a yellow cornucopia spilling with gold coins, all framed by a green wreath.

CAPITAL
Lima

INDEPENDENCE
July 28, 1821

MAJOR CITIES
Lima, Arequipa, Callao, Trujillo, Chiclayo, Piura

DEPARTMENTS
Amazonas, Ancash, Apurímac, Arequipa, Ayacucho, Cajamarca, Callao, Cuzco, Huancavelica, Huánuco, Ica, Junín, La Libertad, Lambayeque, Lima, Loreto, Madre de Dios, Moquegua, Pasco, Piura, Puno, San Martín, Tacna, Tumbes and Ucayali.

POPULATION
28 million (2006 estimate)

MAIN GEOGRAPHIC REGIONS
Costa (western coastal region);
Sierra (central Andes region);
Selva (eastern rain forest region)

HIGHEST POINT
Mount Huascarán at 22,205 feet (6,765 m).

ETHNIC GROUPS
Indigenous 45 percent, mestizo 37 percent, European 15 percent, African, Japanese, Chinese and others 3 percent (2005 estimate)

OFFICIAL LANGUAGES
Spanish and Quechua

LITERACY
91 percent (2005 estimate)

MAIN RELIGION
Roman Catholic (90 percent)

LIFE EXPECTANCY
69 years (2005 estimate)

PUBLIC HOLIDAYS
New Year's Day (January 1); Maundy Thursday (March/April); Good Friday (March/April); Easter (March/April); Labor Day (May 1); Inti Raymi in Cuzco Day (June 24); Saint Peter's and Saint Paul's Day (June 29); Independence Days (2-day festivities) (July 28); Saint Rosa of Lima Day (August 30); Battle of Angamos Day (October 8); All Saints' Day (November 1); Feast of the Immaculate Conception (December 8); Christmas (December 25)

TIME LINE

IN PERU	IN THE WORLD
40,000–15,000 B.C. First Peruvians descended from nomadic tribes during the last Ice Age.	
5000 B.C. Cotton is first cultivated in Peru.	
	753 B.C. Rome is founded.
300 B.C.–A.D. 700 Rise of Nazca cultures; Nazca Lines drawn.	**116–17 B.C.** The Roman empire reaches its greatest extent, under Emperor Trajan (98–17).
A.D. 300 Burial of Mochican leader, Lord of Sipán.	**A.D. 600** Height of Mayan civilization
1200 Manco Cápac becomes the first Incan emperor of the Inca Empire.	**1000** The Chinese perfect gunpowder and begin to use it in warfare.
1438–1493 Reign of Pachacútec; Sacsayhuamán and Machu Picchu are built.	
1527–1533 Division of the Incan empire sparks civil war. Atahualpa gains control of the entire empire but is captured by Spanish conquistador, Francisco Pizarro and assassinated by Spaniards.	**1530** Beginning of transatlantic slave trade organized by the Portuguese in Africa.
1535 Pizarro makes Lima the capital of the Viceroyalty of Peru.	**1558–1603** Reign of Elizabeth I of England.
1572 Tupac Amaru, the last Incan emperor, is captured and executed.	**1620** Pilgrims sail the *Mayflower* to America.
	1776 U.S. Declaration of Independence
1824 Peru defeats Spain and becomes last Latin American colony to gain independence.	**1789–99** The French Revolution
	1861 The U.S. Civil War begins.

IN PERU	IN THE WORLD
	1869 The Suez Canal is opened.
1879–83 Peru defeated in War of the Pacific and loses southern territory to Chile.	**1914** World War I begins.
1941 Peru gains the northern Amazon in the war against Ecuador.	**1939** World War II begins.
	1945 The United States drops atomic bombs on Hiroshima and Nagasaki.
	1966–69 The Chinese Cultural Revolution
1980 Maoist terrorist group Sendero Luminoso (Shining Path) and Tupac Amaru Revolutionary Movement guerrillas start civil war.	
1985–1988 President Alan García Pérez's policies cause hyperinflation and Peru seeks assistance from the International Monetary Fund.	**1986** Nuclear power disaster at Chernobyl in Ukraine
1990 Alberto Fujimori becomes president and institutes severe market reforms.	**1991** Break-up of the Soviet Union
1997 El Niño—the worst of the century—causes severe drought in Peru.	**1997** Hong Kong is returned to China.
2000–2005 Fujimori wins a third 5-year term but political corruption forces him into exile. Alejandro Toledo is Peru's first president of native origin but his term is mired in crisis.	**2001** Terrorists crash planes in New York, Washington, D.C., and Pennsylvania. **2003** War in Iraq
2006 Alan García wins the second round of the Peruvian presidential elections.	

GLOSSARY

aji (a-HE)
A South American chili varying in color from orange-red to yellow or brown.

barrio (BAH-ree-oh)
District, neighborhood, or suburb.

chicha (CHEE-chah)
Beer made from fermented corn.

cholo (CHOH-loh)
Indigenous person trying to join mestizo society.

Creole (kre-ol)
Person of European descent born in Spanish America.

curandero (kur-ahn-DAIR-oh)
A spiritual healer, shaman, or folk doctor.

encomenderos (en-koh-men-DER-ohs)
Local village chiefs in colonial times.

encomienda (en-koh-MYEN-dah)
System instituted by the Spanish colonizers: land was given to a Spaniard, who had the right to force the natives living there to work.

hispanistas (ees-pan-EES-tahs)
Artists using a Spanish-derived style.

huaquero (wah-KAY-roh)
Person who robs precolonial temples, burial sites, or shrines.

indigenistas (een-dee-hain-EES-tahs)
Artists using native subjects for their work.

machismo (mah-CHEES-moh)
Belief in male strength and superiority.

mate (mah-tay)
A kind of herbal tea.

mestizo (mes-TEE-zoh)
Person of mixed Spanish and native origin.

picante (pee-KAHN-tay)
Spicy; a style of cooking spicy foods.

quipu (KEE-poo)
System of knotted string that Incas used for communication.

reducciónes (ray-duc-SYO-nays)
Artificial towns created by Spanish colonizers for native peoples.

Selva
Amazon region east of the Andes.

Sendero Luminoso
(sen-DER-oh loo-mee-NOH-soh)
"Shining Path," a guerrilla group.

shaman
Village healer providing herbal medicine.

Sierra
Mountainous Andes region running through the center of Peru.

FURTHER INFORMATION

BOOKS

Atwood, Roger. *Stealing History: Tomb Raiders, Smugglers, and the Looting of the Ancient World*. New York: St. Martin's Press, 2004.

Burger, Richard L. and Lucy C. Salazar. *Machu Picchu: Unveiling the Mystery of the Incas*. New Haven, CT: Yale University Press, 2004.

Custer, Tony. *The Art of Peruvian Cuisine*. Montreal, QC: Les Editions Ganesha, 2003.

Ferreira, Cesar and Eduardo Dargent-Chamot. *Culture and Customs of Peru*. Wichita, KS: Greenwood Research Books Group, 2002.

Orlove, Ben. *Lines in the Water: Nature and Culture at Lake Titicaca*. Berkeley, CA: University of California Press, 2002.

Thomson, Hugh. *The White Rock: An Exploration of the Inca Heartland*. Woodstock. New York: Overlook Press, 2003.

WEB SITES

"Biodiversity and Protected Areas—Peru" 2003. http://earthtrends.wri.org/ pdf_library/country_profiles/bio_cou_604.pdf

Earth Trends: "Endangered Species: Traded to Death." http://earthtrends.wri.org/features/view_feature.cfm?theme=7&fid=25

Inter Press Service News Agency. "How Much is the Biodiversity of the Andes Worth?" www.ipsnews.net/africa/ interna.asp?idnews=27279

Monga Bay. http://rainforests.mongabay.com/deforestation/2000/Peru.htm

MSN Encarta: "Peru: Environmental Issues." http://encarta.msn.com/encyclopedia_761570790_2/Peru_(country).html

Official Site for the Promotion of Peru: "Gastronomy." www.peru.info/e_ftoculturaeng.asp?pdr=757&jrq=5.5&ic=2&ids=1503

Peru Village: "Peru Biodiversity." www.peruvillage.com/store/biodiversity.html

UNESCO: "World Heritage List." http://whc.unesco.org/en/li

Trade Environment Database (TED) Case Studies: "Peru, Coca Trade, and Environment." www.american.edu/ted/perucoca.htm

BIBLIOGRAPHY

Fisher, John R., ed. *Peru.* Santa Barbara, CA: ABC-CLIO, 1990.

Hudson, Rex A. *Peru, A Country Study.* Washington, D.C.: U.S. Government Printing Office, 1993.

Lepthein, Emilie U. *Peru.* Chicago: Children's Press, 1992.

Lerner Publications Co. *Peru in Pictures.* Minneapolis, MN: Lerner Publications Co., 1992.

Meyerson, Julia. *Tambo: Life in an Andean Village.* Austin, TX: University of Texas Press, 1990.

Norman, Ruth and Charles Spaegel. *The Last Inca—Atahualpa: An Eye-Witness Account of the Conquest of Peru.* El Cajon, CA: Unarius Publications, 1993.

Cultural Expeditions: Culinary History of Peru. www.culturalexpeditions.com/culinary_history.html

Enjoy Peru: The Devil's Last Dance. www.enjoyperu.com/peru_travel_tours_information/conozca_peru_magazine/enjoy_peru_articles/the_devil_last_dance_the_devil_last_dance.html

The Register: Peruvians Develop Super-Tasty Guinea Pig. www.theregister.co.uk/2004/10/19/super_guinea_pig/

WWF in Peru: About the Country. www.panda.org/about_wwf/where_we_work/latin_america_and_caribbean/where/peru/about/index.cfm

INDEX